CW00373318

THE OFFICIAL

Y

YELLOWSTONE

←— BAR BOOK —→

Adams Media
An Imprint of Simon & Schuster, LLC
100 Technology Center Drive
Stoughton, Massachusetts 02072

First Adams Media hardcover edition November 2024

ADAMS MEDIA and colophon are registered trademarks of Simon & Schuster, LLC.

Simon & Schuster: Celebrating 100 Years of Publishing in 2024

For information about special discounts for bulk purchases, please contact Simon & Schuster Special Sales at 1-866-506-1949 or business@simonandschuster.com.

The Simon & Schuster Speakers Bureau can bring authors to your live event. For more information or to book an event, contact the Simon & Schuster Speakers Bureau at 1-866-248-3049 or visit our website at www.simonspeakers.com.

Interior design by Sylvia McArdle
Images © 123RF; Spike Cable Networks Inc.
Cocktail photographs by Harper Point Photography

Manufactured in the United States of America

1 2024

Library of Congress Cataloging-in-Publication Data
Names: Taylor, Lex, author. | Gurr, Nathan, author
Title: The official Yellowstone bar book / Lex Taylor and Nathan Gurr.
Description: First Adams Media hardcover edition. | Stoughton, Massachusetts: Adams Media, 2024. | Includes index.
Identifiers: LCCN 2024019292 | ISBN 9781507222836 (hc) | ISBN 9781507222843 (ebook)
Classification: LCC TX951 .T39 2024 | DDC 641.87/4--dc23/eng/20240517
LC record available at https://lccn.loc.gov/2024019292

ISBN 978-1-5072-2283-6
ISBN 978-1-5072-2284-3 (ebook)

THE OFFICIAL

YELLOWSTONE

— BAR BOOK —

75 COCKTAILS TO ENJOY AFTER THE WORK'S DONE

LEX TAYLOR & NATHAN GURR

ADAMS MEDIA
NEW YORK   LONDON   TORONTO   SYDNEY   NEW DELHI

CONTENTS

Introduction 7

Tools of the Trade 8

CHAPTER 1
STIRRED COCKTAILS 14

CHAPTER 2
SHAKEN COCKTAILS 64

CHAPTER 3
BEER & WINE COCKTAILS 98

CHAPTER 4
SHOTS 132

CHAPTER 5
DIGESTIFS & APERITIFS 164

About the Authors 198

Index 200

INTRODUCTION

When it's time to pour one after a hard day's work, *The Official Yellowstone Bar Book* helps you relax like a Dutton. From the early watering holes along the Oregon Trail in *1883* to the Prohibition speakeasies of *1923* to the bars and campfires of *Yellowstone* and beyond, finding the right drink for the right moment has always been an important part of frontier life. Now you can use the inspiration of your favorite franchise to do just that in the comfort of your own home.

The Official Yellowstone Bar Book features recipes that reflect the characters and themes from *Yellowstone*—as well as the cowboy in all of us. And while it's typically three fingers of bourbon or a beer in the Bunkhouse, this collection includes cocktails you might find in a Bozeman speakeasy, or drop shots you can still find in a favorite like the Crystal Bar, or drinks straight from the Dutton home bar.

It's the perfect collection for drinkers and drink makers with a love for the brand. Whether you've been doing cowboy sh*t all day or are just rewatching your favorite episodes, *The Official Yellowstone Bar Book* serves up the perfect reward.

TOOLS OF THE TRADE

The cowboy lifestyle relies on simple, time-tested tools. It's not about big technology, but a mastery of the basic elements: leather, rope, knots, and confidence that comes with practice. Being a proficient drink maker is no different. There are only a handful of tools you'll need to produce the drinks in this book.

BAR TOOLS

Mixing Glass

A vessel used for cocktails that are stirred as opposed to shaken. The Japanese Yarai mixing glass is the standard in cocktail bars worldwide, but a traditional pint glass also works well.

Metal Shakers

A vessel used for cocktails that require shaking. Boston and cobbler are two examples of shakers commonly used for shaking cocktails. A good shaker is any vessel that seals and allows for vigorous shaking of a cocktail without coming apart and making a mess! Shakers can also be used to mix drinks.

Bar Spoon

Bar spoons come in many shapes, sizes, and styles. They're typically long (usually about 12 inches) to accommodate the reach needed to stir a cocktail in a mixing glass, and their stems are generally rounded or spindled to make the task of stirring a drink easier.

Jigger

Traditionally, a jigger is a unit of measurement equal to 1½ ounces. A jigger is also a tool used to measure ingredients in cocktails. A jigger is typically double-sided with different measurements at each end and comes in many shapes, styles, and sizes. These measurements can range from a fraction of an ounce to several ounces.

Strainer

There are three basic kinds of cocktail strainers: mesh, Hawthorne, and julep. The handheld mesh strainer is cone shaped and used to filter out small ingredient particles with its fine mesh, like a sieve, as you pour the drink through. The Hawthorne strainer is designed to fit over the shaker tin or mixing glass and has a coil around it to help filter fine particles. Finally, the julep strainer is placed inside a mixing glass to keep the ice from being poured into the cocktail glass with the drink.

Wood Chip Smoker and Wood Chips

A cocktail smoker is a device that projects a layer of smoke into a glass and on top of a drink. The simplest forms of cocktail smokers come with wood chips (such as dried cherry or apple wood), are commonly made of wood or clay, and are designed to sit on top of a glass, where the smoker, having been filled with dried wood chips or spices, sends a layer of smoke into the glass when ignited by a pastry torch.

Pastry Torch

A pastry torch is a butane-fueled lighter that is slightly more powerful than a typical lighter. As the name suggests, it is commonly used in pastry kitchens for desserts like crème brûlée. These torches are also useful for tasks such as melting cheese, browning crusts, and even starting fires in a woodstove or fireplace.

Large Ice Cube Molds

Large ice molds come in different sizes and shapes. The purpose of larger ice cubes in a drink is to allow for slower melt. In drinks that are particularly boozy (like the old-fashioned), large ice keeps the drink from becoming watered down too quickly. Unless otherwise noted in the recipe, feel free to use whatever ice you prefer—large cubes, crushed ice, or regular cubes.

GLASSES

Collins

This tall, narrow, cylinder-shaped glass usually holds 10–14 ounces. It is often used to serve mixed drinks that are topped with a sparkling element.

Coupe

The coupe glass is stemmed, usually with a rounded bowl and a wide top. Coupes are used for cocktails that are served "up." In most cocktail bars over the past ten to twenty years, the more traditional coupe has replaced the more modern martini glass as a stylistic preference in regard to the martini cocktail.

Double Rocks

While it may seem like this glass can hold double what a rocks glass can, a double rocks glass can only hold 12–14 ounces of liquid. This glass leaves more room for ice when serving.

Flute

A flute is a tall, stemmed glass that accommodates 4–6 ounces, usually used for champagne or something sparkling.

Martini

The martini glass, or cocktail glass, ranges in size from 4–12 ounces and is cone shaped with a tall stem.

Mug

The two most common mugs used in cocktails are the copper mug, used for mules, and the coffee mug, used for warm drinks. The copper mug holds 14–16 ounces, while the regular coffee mug varies but traditionally holds 8–10 ounces.

Pint

Pint glasses are usually used for beer and specialty drinks, but they can also be used as mixing glasses. They typically hold 16 ounces.

Rocks

The rocks glass is a short tumbler used for most cocktails that are served with ice or straight up (no ice). It can usually accommodate about 4–8 ounces.

Shot Glass

Shot glasses can range in size, but the most common is 1½ ounces. Some can be less than an ounce, and others can be over 3 ounces.

Wine

While there are many kinds of wine glasses, for the purposes of this book, use an all-purpose wine glass of your choosing. Note that wine glasses that are more delicate in nature (and often more expensive) will more easily break when ice is an added ingredient. Act accordingly.

CHAPTER I

STIRRED COCKTAILS

L ike cowboying, preserving the Dutton Ranch is more of a lifestyle than a day job. Every season brings new and bigger challengers, including Thomas Rainwater and the Broken Rock Reservation, claiming the land was stolen from them by early settlers; land developer Dan Jenkins; the scheming and murderous Beck brothers; Market Equities; and even the convict Garrett Randall, who famously said, "Empires aren't bought—they're taken." Though the struggles are constant and the fights plenty, the Duttons have a way of persisting. It may be John's "meaner than evil" attitude, Kayce's warrior instinct, Jamie's knowledge of law, Beth's cunning ruthlessness, or Rip's strong, silent approach. Regardless, when you stir these characters together, you're left with the spirit of the West.

Throughout the seasons of *Yellowstone* and the spin-off series *1883* and *1923*, alcohol plays an important role. Much of the time on the show, the drink is whiskey, straight up or with only simple additions. It's these types of spirit-forward drinks that lend themselves best to stirring. With stirring, you can greatly limit diluting the spirit and keep the focus squarely where it belongs. For cocktails where the spirit or spirits are the focus, such as an old-fashioned, a Manhattan, or a martini, stirring is generally recommended. The process of stirring serves not just to mix the ingredients but to cool and dilute the drink as well.

When stirring a cocktail, the size of the ice is critical. Small bits of ice can quickly melt, overdiluting and overchilling a drink. For stirred cocktails, larger ice cubes are recommended. Stirring can be done in the serving glass, or a drink can be stirred in a mixing glass and then strained into a serving glass either straight up or on the rocks.

CLASSIC OLD-FASHIONED

★ ★ ★

Out-of-towners, greedy land developers, and multibillion-dollar corporations
threaten the old-fashioned way of life in Montana. John Dutton stands firm in
the face of progress. "I am the wall it bashes against, and I will not be the one
who breaks." This classic drink of bitters, sugar, and whiskey predates the word
"cocktail." When cocktails became popular and more complex in the 1850s,
some patrons would ask for this drink. A classic, even then.

Serves I

¼ ounce Demerara syrup

2 dashes Angostura bitters

2 ounces bourbon

1 orange twist

1 cocktail cherry

I. In a mixing glass, combine Demerara syrup, bitters,
and bourbon. Add ice and stir for 15 seconds.

2. Strain into a rocks glass over a large ice cube.
Garnish with orange twist and cocktail cherry.

═ The Multifaceted Old-Fashioned ═

*The old-fashioned hasn't ever really been out of fashion. It's
considered a foundational drink in the world of cocktails. In
fact, you can vary the flavor of the drink simply by changing
the type of whiskey, adding a different sweetener, or changing
the bitters. For example, in Yellowstone, Buffalo Trace bourbon
and Weller Special Reserve bourbon both make appearances.
By simply switching the two whiskeys, the flavor profile and
texture of the drink changes.*

YELLOWSTONE RANCH OLD-FASHIONED

★ ★ ★

As Dan Jenkins says in *Yellowstone*, Season 1, Episode 1, "Every millionaire I know wants to be a cowboy—authenticity is the one thing money can't buy." In *Yellowstone*, authenticity is key. Whether bull riding, barrel racing, or drinking it up at the bar, it's all about being true to the craft. This drink uses Weller Special Reserve wheated bourbon, a whiskey enjoyed by the Duttons.

Serves I

¼ ounce Demerara syrup

3 dashes Angostura bitters

2 dashes orange bitters

2 ounces Weller Special Reserve bourbon

In a mixing glass, combine Demerara syrup, bitters, and bourbon. Add ice and stir for 15 seconds, then strain over a large ice cube in a rocks glass.

★

Bar Note

Weller Special Reserve is the world's first wheated bourbon. Wheated bourbons tend to have a more delicate note than most other bourbons that contain rye. To make a comparison to the wine world, while high-rye bourbons generally parallel heavier, spicier wines such as Syrah, wheated bourbons have softer, lighter notes like pinot noir.

PIONEER
OLD-FASHIONED

★ ★ ★

In Episode 4 of *1883*, Captain Shea leads the European immigrants as they prepare the wagons to cross the Brazos River. After finding all kinds of useless belongings weighing down the wagons, he says, "I said, if it is not absolutely necessary, it does not make the trip." Referring to a piano, Josef replies, "It is necessary. He is a musician." Shea replies, "No! He is not a musician, and you are not a carpenter, and he's not a f*cking blacksmith. You're pioneers, and that's all you are until you get there." Like a pioneer, mix your whiskey with leftover bacon fat from the chuck wagon before making the crossing. It beats losing it to the river.

Serves I

2 ounces bacon-fat-washed bourbon (see Fat Washing sidebar in this chapter)

3 dashes Angostura bitters

2 dashes orange bitters

¼ ounce honey syrup (see Bee's Knees in Chapter 2)

1 cocktail cherry

1 orange twist

I. In a mixing glass, combine bourbon, bitters, and honey syrup. Add ice and stir for 15 seconds.

2. Strain over a large ice cube in a rocks glass and garnish with cocktail cherry and orange twist.

★

≡ Use Large Ice Cubes ≡

In the past handful of years, you may have noticed more and more cocktail bars using large ice cubes in some of their cocktails, or for select spirits ordered on the rocks without mixers. The reason large cubes are used is because they tend to melt more slowly. The more slowly the drink melts, the longer the person imbibing has time to enjoy the drink's balance.

Fat Washing

Elevate any drink game by fat washing your booze. It's easy to do, and chances are you've already got some flavorful stuff to use at home. Try experimenting with bacon, brown butter, trimmings from a smoked brisket, pork jowl, and even coconut fat. Nothing is off-limits. You can fat wash any liquor, but whiskey and dark rum are the most popular.

A good rule is to use 1 part fat to 10 parts liquor. But you can use more fat, especially if time is a concern and you're looking to quickly impart more flavor. Your fat doesn't have to be clarified, and burned bits are fine, especially since they will all be filtered out at the end. Just note that the smoothness and flavor of your fat will impart into the final spirit, so it's better to use fats without burned or creosote notes. Here's how to do it:

I. Mix 1:10 rendered fat with whiskey (or a spirit of your choice) in a bottle. Shake and then let sit at room temperature for 24 hours. Again, this can be less time with more fat. Shake every so often.

2. Once you're ready to filter, place the bottle into the freezer for at least 3 hours. The fat will freeze and separate from the booze.

3. Remove the large chunks of fat either by hand or through a strainer.

4. Place a coffee filter in a strainer and slowly pour your mixture through it into a container large enough to hold the amount of liquor you have. You will find it takes time for the mixture to filter. If you're filtering lots of booze, change out the coffee filter for a fresh one halfway through the process. Once properly filtered, liquor will be shelf stable.

CLASSIC MANHATTAN

★ ★ ★

When city folk started buying up second homes in Montana, they brought a few drinks with them. And though their presence may not always be welcome, this drink is at home wherever you find it. Spend a little extra of your week's wages to garnish with a cocktail cherry or two.

Serves I

2 dashes Angostura bitters
1 ounce sweet vermouth
2 ounces rye or bourbon
1 cocktail cherry

In a mixing glass, combine bitters, vermouth, and whiskey. Add ice to the glass and stir for 20 seconds. Strain into a martini glass and garnish with cocktail cherry.

▬ On the Rocks ▬

The Manhattan is a classic, whether straight up or on the rocks. If your preference is for rocks, you may want to stir in a little less ice because the ice in the glass will further dilute the drink as it's sipped.

MANHATTAN'S BLACK HEART

★ ★ ★

Kayce refers to city folk as "transplants" because, as he tells it, they are "people that come and try to make this place just like the one they left." This conflict between two very different ways of life is at the core of *Yellowstone*. Yet this beautiful black drink would be right at home in one of Bozeman's upscale bars, so not every change leads to conflict. To make your own Guinness syrup, combine 2 ounces Guinness with 2 ounces white sugar in a small saucepan. Place it over medium heat and stir until sugar dissolves. Allow to cool before using.

──────────────── Serves I ────────────────

⅛ teaspoon activated charcoal

½ ounce Guinness syrup

3 dashes chocolate mole bitters

2 ounces bourbon

1 cocktail cherry

1 orange twist

I. In a mixing glass, combine activated charcoal, Guinness syrup, bitters, and bourbon. Add ice and stir for 15 seconds.

2. Strain over a large ice cube in a rocks glass and garnish with cocktail cherry and orange twist.

Using Activated Charcoal

You can buy activated charcoal in most grocery stores and drugstores. It's worth noting that it has the effect of neutralizing medications because it acts as a filter. In bars and restaurants, you'll often see an asterisk on the menu with a similar caveat.

PHANTOM PAIN
(BETH'S MARTINI)

★ ★ ★

After her falling out with Bob, Beth meets him and his assistant at the bar. She orders a double Tito's with three olives. The waiter says, "You mean a martini?" Beth replies, "No, martinis have vermouth and are enjoyed with friends. I don't like vermouth, and these aren't my friends." Throughout the series, Beth often drinks some version of a martini, changing up the basics to suit her mood. Though a proper martini would be stirred, Beth's version is simply poured into the glass and served.

Serves I

3 ounces Tito's Handmade Vodka

3 skewered olives

Place a large ice cube in a rocks glass, add vodka, and garnish with olives.

══ Watch Those Measurements ══

From town to town, state to state, and country to country, measurements in cocktails may vary slightly. A "double Tito's" may mean a whopping 4 ounces of straight booze in some establishments. Many bars consider 1½ ounces to be a full pour, while others consider 2 ounces a full pour. There are even some places that distinguish a jiggered pour (traditionally 1½ ounces as a unit of measurement, not to be confused with the tool also referred to as a "jigger") from a "neat" pour of 2 ounces.

MODERN MARTINI

★ ★ ★

Though simple in its ingredients, the martini is one of the most nuanced cocktails. There's a fine line between good and bad. Just like Yellowstone itself, this drink achieves authenticity through a delicate balance of the bold and the nuanced. When serving a martini, pay special attention to the details. This can also be served in a coupe glass and you can forgo the standard olives and garnish with a fruit twist or a few drops of olive oil.

Serves I

3/4 ounce dry vermouth

3 ounces gin

3 olives for garnish

I. In a mixing glass, combine vermouth and gin. Add ice and stir for 20 seconds.

2. Using a julep strainer, strain into a chilled martini glass.

3. Garnish with olives.

★

≡ The Martini ≡

Martini presentation is a big deal in the world of cocktails. How a bartender handles the nature of a martini says almost as much about the bartender as it does about the guest who ordered it. There's history, there are little pro tips here and there, and there might even be a story or two.

The modern martini has shifted in the past decade. With the explosion of new quality gins and vodkas on the market in the early 2000s, some cocktail bars would simply leave out the vermouth without even asking the person who ordered it how they preferred their martini. In the 2010s, savvy bartenders became increasingly familiar with a number of high-quality vermouths, and so currently, a guest may or may not be asked their preference from bar to bar.

Here are some notes on martini lingo (also note that the lingo may differ depending on where you go):

- "Straight up" implies no vermouth.
- "Very dry" usually implies no vermouth.
- "On the dry side" implies roughly $1/2$ ounce of vermouth.
- "In and out" implies coating the martini glass with vermouth and then dumping it out before straining the cocktail into the glass.
- "Dirty" implies $1/2$ ounce of olive juice (usually this means no vermouth).
- "Extra dirty" implies $3/4$ ounce of olive juice.
- "Filthy" implies 1 full ounce of olive juice.
- "Dirty ice on the side" implies that regardless of how the drink is prepared, the ice used to stir the martini will be offered in a rocks glass alongside the martini itself.
- "Straight up on the rocks with a little vermouth" implies that the person is either confused or drunk. Act accordingly.

RANCH WATER

★ ★ ★

In Season 4, Episode 4 of *Yellowstone*, Travis tells Jimmy in the truck heading to Texas, "When the Sixes is done with you, you'll spend the rest of your life on one [horse], or never get on another one." That's the way of the ranch. Likewise, this simple and refreshing drink is the way of many Texas ranches and is likely one you'll never get off of.

Serves 1

3/4 ounce lime juice

2 ounces tequila

4 ounces Topo Chico sparkling water

1 lime wedge

Fill a collins glass with your preferred ice. Add lime juice and tequila and top with sparkling water. Stir for a quick 2 seconds to combine the ingredients. Garnish with lime wedge.

GIN RICKEY

★ ★ ★

The Gin Rickey is a citrusy and refreshing drink that was featured in the Bozeman speakeasy in Season 1, Episode 3 of *1923*. Jack asks what the fancy people are drinking, and the bartender serves Gin Rickeys. Needless to say, Elizabeth is impressed.

Serves I

3/4 ounce lime juice

2 ounces gin

4 ounces soda water

1 lime wedge

Fill a collins glass with your preferred ice. Add lime juice and gin to the glass and top with soda water. Stir for a quick 2 seconds to combine the ingredients. Garnish with lime wedge.

IRON IN THE FIRE

★ ★ ★

In Season 4, Episode 5 of *Yellowstone*, "Under a Blanket of Red," Beth sits at the breakfast table with John. When he asks what she's working on, she replies that she has "a few irons in the fire," which means that one or two people are about to have a bad day. This cocktail gently pairs delicate cherry wood smoke with maple syrup to brighten up any bad day.

Serves I

¼ ounce smoked maple syrup

3 dashes Angostura bitters

2 dashes orange bitters

1 ounce bourbon

1 ounce Armagnac

1 cocktail cherry

Cherry wood chips for smoking

I. In a mixing glass, combine maple syrup, bitters, bourbon, and Armagnac. Add ice and stir for 15 seconds.

2. Strain over a large ice cube in a rocks glass. Garnish with cocktail cherry and cherry wood smoke.

★

Beautiful Bitters

Don't be afraid of bitters. If you don't like the taste, you don't have to use them. If you happen to like the taste, be confident with your dashes of bitters. Bitters give structure and depth to a cocktail's profile. And luckily, there are plenty of bitters out there to try. Just don't try your hand with a bitter Bunkhouse boy. Tends not to end well.

Building, Dressing, and Accessorizing Cocktails

When building a cocktail in a mixing glass, a shaker, or the glass itself, start with the cheapest ingredient and work up from there. That way, if you make a mistake, there is little downside: It's better to throw out a bit of lemon juice or simple syrup rather than the more expensive spirits that make up most of the drink. It's also good practice to add ice after combining ingredients. If for some reason there is a pause in making a drink, or perhaps you are making more than one drink at a time, waiting to add ice until the drinks are ready to shake or stir will ensure that a cocktail isn't melting away. Here are a few other ways to accessorize your cocktail:

- **Smoking cocktails:** *Smoking cocktails is becoming more and more common. There are many cocktail smokers on the market, and the simplest ones are usually preferred. The idea of smoking cocktails is to infuse the first sip or two with a smoky flavor. The smoke itself adds an aesthetic to the cocktail as well as a fragrance. If a garnish is a cocktail's jewelry, think of the smoke as its cologne or perfume.*

- **Smoked syrups:** *With a cocktail smoker, making smoked syrups is quite simple. After a syrup is made and preferably while it's still warm, strain it into a Mason jar. Smoke the Mason jar and put the lid on before the smoke escapes, and then let it sit. The longer it sits, the smokier the flavor. Also, the more surface area of the syrup that is exposed to the smoke, the better the result. Sometimes laying the jar on its side helps this process along.*

RIP ROY

★ ★ ★

This is a take on the classic Rob Roy cocktail, a drink dating back to the late 1800s. It's similar to a Manhattan except that it features Scotch instead of rye or bourbon, which gives it a distinct smoky (or peaty) note. The base of this drink is split with mezcal to give it an extra punch of character.

Just like Rip, this drink is tough and won't back down.

Serves I

1 ounce Scotch

1 ounce mezcal

1 ounce sweet vermouth

2 dashes Angostura bitters

2 moonshine cherries

I. In a mixing glass, combine Scotch, mezcal, vermouth, and bitters. Add ice and stir for 15 seconds.

2. Strain over a large ice cube in a rocks glass, and garnish with moonshine cherries.

≡ Cattle Branding ≡

Livestock branding can be traced back to drawings almost five thousand years old in Egyptian tombs. Spaniards brought the tradition to the Americas in the 1500s, but the act of branding as we know it gained traction in the American West after the Civil War. During the 1800s, a boom in the US population propelled the demand for beef. With more and more cattle roaming the Great Plains, from Texas to Montana, it became paramount to distinguish ownership. Unlike in earlier instances, branding contained mostly letters that included serifs as well as unique modifiers. Brand inspectors helped ensure that brands were registered and unique.

BOURBON BUCK

★ ★ ★

In Season 2, Episode 1 of *Yellowstone*, while Jimmy and Avery talk it up at the bar, a guy asks Avery to dance. Jimmy tells him to f*ck off, which of course turns into an all-out bar brawl. The wranglers decide revenge is a dish best served hot, so they return to the bar with a steer, which they let loose on the place. With refreshing ginger and a steer's kick of bourbon, this drink will loosen you up for your own lively night on the town.

Serves I

½ ounce lemon juice

2 ounces bourbon

6 ounces ginger ale

1 lemon wedge

Fill a collins glass with your preferred ice and add lemon juice and bourbon. Top with ginger ale. Stir for a quick 2 seconds to combine the ingredients. Garnish with lemon wedge.

≡ The Buck ≡

"Bucks" were popular drinks during the early part of the cocktail boom in the nineteenth century. The buck, by nature, is simply a style of drink that can have lemon or lime and ginger ale or ginger beer. Bucks are also perfectly fine with any base spirit. Try a gin buck with lemon and ginger ale, or a tequila buck with lime and ginger beer. Variety in bucks is part of their charm. One theory about the origin of the name "buck" is that it was derived from a simple glass of ginger ale with lemon, referred to as the "horse's neck." Someone added booze, which gave it a "kick" or "buck."

★

≡ Buster Welch ≡

In Season 4 of Yellowstone, *Jimmy is sent to the Four Sixes Ranch in Texas, where, unbeknownst to him, he has the honor of listening to a story from Buster Welch himself. Later, one of the ranch hands tells Jimmy, "There's three gods in Texas—the Almighty Himself, Buster Welch, and George Straight. You just met one of them." Buster Welch passed away in 2022 shortly after being featured in* Yellowstone. *Buster was an inductee into several Halls of Fame, including the Texas Cowboy Hall of Fame. As a child, he would often skip school to ride horses, namely broncos. He left home at the age of thirteen and worked with Foy and Leonard Proctor, learning various ranch chores including riding, breaking horses, and managing cattle. He went on to work at several famous Texas ranches, including many years at the Four Sixes Ranch. He became famous for training cutting horses, which are used to "cut" cattle away from the herd.*

KNIFE'S TIP

★ ★ ★

In *1883*, Episode 8, after helping Captain Shea and his outfit survive a gunfight with horse thieves, thief hunter Charles "Charlie" Goodnight, played by Taylor Sheridan, asks Shea, "Come across any barbed wire yet?" Upon learning Shea has never heard of it, he explains, "It's twisted steel wire with little barbs woven into it. Sharp as a knife's tip. It is the one fence cattle will not push through." This drink has a barbed, sharp taste as well, with the anise and fennel notes of the absinthe mixing with the snappy ginger ale.

Serves 1

1½ ounces absinthe

2 ounces ginger ale

2 ounces prosecco

1 lime wedge

Combine absinthe, ginger ale, and prosecco in a rocks glass with a large ice cube. Stir for a quick 2 seconds to combine the mixture. Garnish with lime wedge.

LONG BLACK TRAIN

★ ★ ★

It usually doesn't end well for enemies of the ranch. Sometimes, the only thing left for them is a trip to the "train station." There is no literal train, nor station; after a shooting, hanging, choking, or rattlesnake to the face, getting taken to the train station involves a steep canyon drop. And as Lloyd says, "At the bottom of that canyon is how the West was won." This black drink with a red cherry is a nod to the long black train, and to all who have ridden it.

◆———————————— Serves I ————————————◆

¼ teaspoon activated charcoal

½ ounce Guinness syrup (see Manhattan's Black Heart in this chapter)

3 dashes Angostura bitters

2 dashes orange bitters

2 ounces rye whiskey

Luxardo cherry juice

Cherry wood chips for smoking

1 Luxardo cherry

I. In a mixing glass, combine charcoal, Guinness syrup, bitters, and whiskey. Add ice and stir for 15 seconds. Strain over a large ice cube in a rocks glass.

2. Smear a layer of cherry juice just below and inside the rim of the rocks glass to give it a dripping-blood effect.

3. Using a cocktail smoker placed directly on top of the glass, add cherry wood smoke, then garnish with cherry.

DRUGSTORE ROOT BEER

★ ★ ★

In the first episode of Season 1 of *1923*, a gentleman at the bar requests "real root beer" and is advised to find it at the drugstore. This decadent and peppery drink is just what the doctor ordered.

———————————— **Serves I** ————————————

2 ounces dark rum

1 ounce bourbon cream

3 dashes chocolate mole bitters

4 ounces root beer

1 cocktail cherry

I. Fill a collins glass with your favorite ice and add rum, bourbon cream, and bitters. Top the glass with root beer.

2. Pour the drink's contents into a mixing glass and then pour it back into the collins glass. Garnish with cocktail cherry.

≡ **Rolling with It** ≡

The technique of pouring a drink back and forth between vessels is also known as "rolling" a cocktail.

HEARTLESS COWGIRL

★ ★ ★

With barbecue bitters, habanero cola, and white corn liquor, this rough but loyal drink will have you falling in love. But be careful, she may hurt your pride. That's a lesson Lloyd learns the hard way when Laramie leaves him for Walker. It's a drink worth the heartbreak.

Serves I

1½ ounces Buffalo Trace White Dog (or moonshine)

1½ ounces amaro

¼ ounce habanero cola syrup

4 dashes barbecue bitters

Hickory chips for smoking

1 lemon twist

I. Rinse a double rocks glass with water.

2. Place one large cube of ice in the glass. In a mixing glass, add Buffalo Trace White Dog, amaro, habanero cola syrup, and bitters. Add ice and stir for 30 seconds.

3. Strain into the double rocks glass. Using a cocktail smoker placed directly on top of the glass, add hickory wood smoke and then garnish with a lemon twist.

CAROLYN'S
WHISKEY PUNCH

★ ★ ★

In Episode 6 of *1883*, Margaret meets Carolyn, a shop owner in Doan's Crossing. With her ice running out, Carolyn offers Margaret some cold whiskey punch to enjoy with her—a real treat after all they've been through. Create a bowl of this punch for your outfit.

———— **Serves 8 (8-ounce glasses)** ————

16 ounces whiskey

20 ounces lemonade

6 ounces honey syrup (see Bee's Knees in Chapter 2)

16 ounces flavored seltzer of your choice

8 blood orange wheels

Combine all ingredients in a punch bowl and stir. Serve in a glass over your preferred ice, garnished with blood orange wheel.

HIGH PLAINS SAZERAC

★ ★ ★

In Episode 9 of *1883*, Elsa narrates, "If land could have emotions, this land hates. It hates us, and everyone can feel it." This classic drink, developed in the mid-1800s, would have been familiar to the early pioneers heading west, and its soothing effects might have made the experience more forgiving.

Serves 1

2 ounces rye whiskey

2 dashes Peychaud's bitters

¼ ounce Demerara syrup

½ ounce absinthe

1 lemon rind

1. Chill a rocks glass with ice water.

2. In a mixing glass, combine whiskey, bitters, and Demerara syrup. Add ice and stir for 20 seconds.

3. Dump ice water out of the rocks glass and add absinthe. Coat the inside of the glass with absinthe, dump it out, and strain contents of the mixing glass into the coated glass.

4. Spritz the glass with lemon rind, then throw rind away.

Sazerac History

The classic Sazerac cocktail is the official cocktail of New Orleans, due to its long history with the city. A Creole apothecary named Anton Peychaud is generally thought to have created the Sazerac in 1838, using his bitters (Peychaud's bitters) and his favorite brandy, the Sazerac de Forge & Fils. The recipe became so popular that a bar called the Sazerac Coffee House started buying Peychaud's bitters and began serving the cocktail. Later the coffee house (which changed its name to the Sazerac House) would buy the rights to the bitters, and its new proprietor, Thomas Handy, then substituted the brandy with an American whiskey.

Later in 1873, an absinthe rinse was added to the Sazerac cocktail. It is said that the absinthe adds a deeper layer of flavor complexity. However, when absinthe was outlawed in 1912 other anise-flavored liqueurs like Herbsaint were substituted in.

The official and trademarked recipe from the Sazerac House is:

1½ ounces Sazerac rye whiskey

1 sugar cube

3 dashes Peychaud's bitters

¼ ounce Herbsaint

1 lemon peel

1. *Fill an old-fashioned glass with ice.*

2. *In a second old-fashioned glass, add sugar cube and bitters. Crush the sugar cube. Add whiskey to the glass. Add ice and stir.*

3. *Empty the ice from the first glass and coat the glass with Herbsaint. Dump remaining Herbsaint.*

4. *Strain whiskey/bitters mixture into the coated glass. Garnish with lemon peel.*

While the recipe that we provide does not follow the exact dictates of the trademark, the ingredients that we recommend are far more readily available.

STARRY NIGHT

★ ★ ★

In Season 2, Episode 7 of *Yellowstone*, Beth and Rip share a bottle of Southern Comfort while sitting on the roof of the ranch. Beth says, "I'll sip whiskey and stare at the stars with you, Rip." She goes on to explain, "I think heaven's right here. So's hell. One person can be walking the clouds right next to someone enduring eternal damnation. And God is the land." This Southern Comfort drink uses heavenly marshmallow syrup and devilish chocolate bitters to achieve a light sweetness with notes of pastry.

Serves I

¼ ounce marshmallow syrup

3 dashes chocolate bitters

½ ounce Southern Comfort

1½ ounces high-rye bourbon

3 small marshmallows, skewered

I. In a mixing glass, combine marshmallow syrup, chocolate bitters, Southern Comfort, and bourbon. Add ice to the mixing glass and stir for 15 seconds.

2. Strain over a large ice cube in a rocks glass. Place skewered marshmallows across the rim of the glass, then light them on fire with a pastry torch. Instruct the imbiber to blow out the flames prior to drinking.

Make Your Own Marshmallow Syrup

First, heavily toast 6 marshmallows with a pastry torch or over a stove flame. In a small saucepan over medium heat, mix ½ cup sugar with ½ cup water and add toasted marshmallows. Simmer until sugar and marshmallow dissolve, about 2 minutes. Allow to cool and then strain before using.

CHAPTER 2

SHAKEN COCKTAILS

Riding rodeo, breaking colts, driving steer—it's all just another day on the ranch for the cowboys of *Yellowstone*. Often at the Bunkhouse, Ryan, Colby, and Lloyd can be found playing poker while Walker sings a sad song. When barrel racers Mia and Laramie join the Bunkhouse in Season 2, it's a recipe for even more good times and strong drinks—and definitely shakes things up.

Shaking up a cocktail is no different. Unlike stirring to prepare a cocktail, vigorously shaking with ice will chill, dilute, and add air to the mix. Usually, a mesh strainer and Hawthorne strainer are used together when pouring into a serving glass. These strainers help remove small shards of ice, pulp, and seeds.

When shaking a cocktail, add your ingredients to the shaker, then add enough ice to fully cover the liquids. Firmly seal the lid and shake vigorously for 15–20 seconds over your shoulder while keeping both hands on the opposite ends of the shaker.

COWBOYS AND DREAMERS

★ ★ ★

"You're either born a willow or born an oak," says Lloyd in Season 3, Episode 5 of *Yellowstone*. Lloyd is a straight shooter, and he's got a way with words. That comes from a lifetime of wearing the brand and living by it on the Dutton Ranch. Like Lloyd, this drink is a good balance of rough but tender, as the olive oil mellows the bite. It's a willow *and* an oak.

Serves I

1 (¼-inch thick) orange round, cut in half

4 large fresh basil leaves, divided

½ ounce Demerara syrup

¼ ounce olive oil

2 ounces vodka or gin

I. In a shaker, muddle half an orange round and 3 basil leaves.

2. Add Demerara syrup, olive oil, and vodka or gin. Then add ice and shake for 20 seconds.

3. Double strain over your preferred ice into a rocks glass and garnish with remaining orange round and basil leaf.

≡ Use Quality Oil ≡

The better the olive oil, the better the drink. In this cocktail, the olive oil will create an oil slick on the surface, which moisturizes your lips as you sip.

BEE'S KNEES

★ ★ ★

In *1923*, Season 1, Episode 3, Elizabeth Strafford drinks a Bee's Knees while admiring the couples dancing at the speakeasy. She asks Jack if he knows the dance. "I don't even know this song," he replies. Though Jack may be out of his element, the Bee's Knees is always right at home. This drink has a beautiful balance between sweet and sour and looks classy in a coupe glass.

Serves I

¾ ounce lemon juice
¾ ounce honey syrup
2 ounces gin
1 lemon twist

In a cocktail shaker, add lemon juice, honey syrup, and gin. Add ice and shake for 15 seconds. Strain into a coupe glass and garnish with lemon twist.

≡ Honey Syrup ≡

To make your own honey syrup, combine equal parts honey and water in a small saucepan, and heat over medium heat until honey dissolves, about 2 minutes. Allow to cool before using. The reason a syrup must be made when using honey—instead of using the honey straight—is that unless you cut down the viscosity of honey, it will stick to the sides of the glass and shaker. The moment regular honey hits ice, it clumps. You don't want your Bee's Knees creaky.

The Classic Bee's Knees

The Gin Rickey and the Bee's Knees, both seen in Season 1 of 1923, are considered classic cocktails. The Rickey cocktail came first in an era spanning the better part of the nineteenth century known as the "Golden Age of Cocktails." The Bee's Knees cocktail is from the era of drinks referred to as "Prohibition Cocktails." These are just two of the classic cocktails covered in this book, which include the daiquiri, which falls somewhere between the Rickey and the Bee's Knees, as well as the Manhattan and martini.

Classic cocktails like the Bee's Knees have been inspiring drinks ever since their inception. The Gold Rush cocktail is an example of what many now consider a modern classic cocktail directly inspired by the Bee's Knees.

STING OF WISDOM

★ ★ ★

In Season 3, Episode 8 of *Yellowstone*, Lloyd tells Rip, "You know, you did something that no one does, Rip. You've outlived your past." Most of the ranch hands on *Yellowstone* have some troubled pasts. For them, working the ranch is a new beginning, an opportunity to wear the brand and to join a family. Like the sizzle of the brand, this spicy bourbon drink carries a sweet sting but goes down smooth, signaling good times to come.

Serves I

3/4 ounce lemon juice
3/4 ounce spicy honey syrup
2 ounces bourbon
1 lemon twist

In a cocktail shaker, add lemon juice, honey syrup, and bourbon. Add ice and shake for 15 seconds. Strain into a coupe glass and garnish with lemon twist.

★

Spicy Honey Syrup

You can choose from plenty of spicy honey syrups on the store shelves. Or you can make it at home with jalapeño. Slice 2 jalapeños and muddle them in a small saucepan. Add 1/2 cup water and 1/2 cup honey. Place over medium heat and simmer until the honey dissolves, about 2 minutes. Allow to cool. Strain the syrup to remove the muddled peppers.

CARA'S THREAT

★ ★ ★

In Season 1, Episode 4 of *1923*, Cara Dutton threatens Banner by saying, "Men kill with bullets or a noose, which is to say men kill quick. Your fight is with me now. I kill much slower." After Jacob is gunned down, Cara takes the reins of the Dutton Ranch. Her refreshing approach to her family and the ranch is both sweet and sour. This refreshing drink is both sweet and sour too.

Serves 1

1 (2-inch) cube watermelon

1 slice cucumber

¾ ounce lemon juice

¾ ounce simple syrup

2 ounces vodka

4 ounces soda water

1. Muddle watermelon cube and cucumber in a cocktail shaker. Add lemon juice, simple syrup, and vodka. Add ice and shake for 20 seconds.

2. Strain into a rocks glass filled with your preferred ice and top with soda water.

CLASSIC
MODERN DAIQUIRI

★ ★ ★

In *1923*, Season 1, Episode 2, Prince Arthur, the Earl of Sussex, says in his engagement speech about Alex, "Allow me to raise a glass to this most unique of locations for the presentation of an engagement. But when you consider the bride, perhaps the company of lions makes perfect sense. After all, she shares their spirit, and their mane." Like Alex, the modern daiquiri is tart yet fiercely refreshing. It serves as the perfect drink for a distinguished crowd.

Serves I

3/4 ounce Demerara syrup

3/4 ounce lime juice

2 ounces rum

1 lime wedge

In a cocktail shaker, combine Demerara syrup, lime juice, and rum. Add ice and shake for 15 seconds. Strain into a coupe glass and garnish with lime wedge.

★

Change Your Rum

You can choose from an incredible variety of rums on the market. Rum is made from molasses, cane honey, or sugar cane. It can be aged like whiskey, and like whiskey, there are many stories revolving around the first rum produced. So be an explorer and seek out different rums. Simply switching the rum in the standard daiquiri recipe can make a noticeable difference in the cocktail's flavor profile.

PRIZE FIGHTER

★ ★ ★

Rip has a rule: Any fighting on the ranch has to be with *him*. And he holds people to that. Whether he's fighting his best man Lloyd, his Bunkhouse boy Walker, or Kayce Dutton over who runs the operation, Rip knows how to throw (and take) a punch. This bloodred drink honors that, achieving its rich color through beet juice ice cubes balanced with mint syrup.

Serves I

3 beet juice ice cubes

6 large mint leaves

1 ounce mint syrup (see No Such Thing as Fair in Chapter 3)

1 ounce lemon juice

2 ounces vodka

1 ounce soda water

1 mint sprig

I. Prep a collins glass by alternating regular ice cubes with beet juice ice cubes.

2. In a cocktail shaker, muddle mint leaves with mint syrup. Add lemon juice and vodka. Add ice to the shaker and shake for 15 seconds.

3. Add soda water to the shaker and then double strain into the prepared collins glass. Garnish with mint sprig.

≡ Make Your Own ≡

To make your own beet juice ice cubes: Fill an ice cube tray two-thirds full with water. Squeeze a wedge or two of lemon over the tops of the cubes and top off with beet juice. Freeze.

LIQUID COURAGE

★ ★ ★

This invigorating take on a gin and tonic is perfect for an afternoon in the sun watching a rodeo. And if you're riding like Jimmy, you might even take a few sips of Liquid Courage before you go. To elevate this to a cooling refreshment, try freezing the grapes you use for garnishes.

Serves I

4 Cotton Candy grapes, divided

2 (1-inch) rosemary sprigs, divided

¾ ounce lime juice

½ ounce simple syrup

1½ ounces gin

4 ounces tonic water

I. In a cocktail shaker, muddle 3 grapes and 1 rosemary sprig. Add lime juice, simple syrup, and gin. Add ice and shake for 15 seconds.

2. Double strain into a collins glass over your preferred ice. Top with tonic water and garnish with remaining grape skewered on remaining rosemary sprig.

Try New Tonics

Gin and tonics have enjoyed a surge due to a plethora of quality tonics (and gins) now available on the market. There are also a growing number of flavored tonics that you could try in this recipe. This cocktail can take on a whole new flavor profile with a different tonic, so have fun experimenting.

COWBOY JULEP

★ ★ ★

In *Yellowstone*, Season 4, Episode 10, Jimmy describes to Lloyd his experience at the Four Sixes Ranch: "It's just cattle and cowboys all the way to the horizon." They're talking about how, in Texas, you don't have to fight the whole world to do your job, because your neighbor has the same one. This means that after a long day of roping cattle, there's no problem inviting over your neighbors for some ice-cold, refreshing juleps. Maybe you want to give that a try?

— Serves I —

5 mint leaves

½ ounce cayenne honey syrup

2 ounces Buffalo Trace bourbon

1 mint sprig

I. In a cocktail shaker, lightly muddle mint leaves and cayenne honey syrup together. Add bourbon and ice and shake for 15 seconds.

2. Double strain over crushed ice in a rocks glass and garnish with mint sprig.

≡ Making Cayenne Syrup ≡

Making your own cayenne syrup is easy: In a small saucepan over medium heat, add equal parts honey and water. Add cayenne to taste (roughly ¼ teaspoon per half cup liquid). Simmer for 2 minutes and then allow to cool.

★

≡ Buffalo Trace Whiskey ≡

Buffalo Trace bourbon from the Buffalo Trace Distillery in Frankfort, Kentucky, is a high-rye bourbon that predates the United States itself. As an entry-level bourbon in a line of whiskeys that includes highly sought-after expressions such as Blanton's, William Larue Weller, and Pappy Van Winkle (to name only a few), Buffalo Trace bourbon stands alone in its quality. For anyone desiring a taste of a highly respected and quintessential bourbon, Buffalo Trace is it when it comes to high-rye bourbons. An interesting thing to consider is that Weller Special Reserve—also consumed in Yellowstone—is the quintessential wheated bourbon and is also part of the Buffalo Trace line. When Maker's Mark (a staple wheated bourbon in bars) wanted to create their mash bill, legend has it that they consulted Weller before doing so.

SPICY SUMMER

★ ★ ★

In Season 5, Episode 5 of *Yellowstone*, Gator is at a loss for what to prepare for Summer, who doesn't eat gluten, dairy, or meat. Beth tells Gator to go out in the field and serve her up some grass. But not everything vegan needs to be tasteless. This vegan drink is fresh and spicy enough to please even Summer…or Beth, for that matter.

◆──────────────── Serves I ────────────────◆

3 slices jalapeño, divided

2 cilantro sprigs, divided

¾ ounce simple syrup

¾ ounce lime juice

2 ounces rum

¼ ounce apple cider vinegar

1. Muddle 2 jalapeño slices and 1 cilantro sprig in a cocktail shaker.

2. Add simple syrup, lime juice, rum, and ice and shake vigorously for 15 seconds.

3. Double strain over a large ice cube in rocks glass. Stir in apple cider vinegar and then garnish with remaining cilantro and jalapeño.

TWISTER

★ ★ ★

On the trail, pioneers faced endless struggles. However, few were as dark and ominous as a massive tornado. That may be why, years later, Beth Dutton refers to herself as one that tears through a trailer park. This twist on a Dark 'n Stormy uses cream soda to emphasize that dark and ominous look.

Serves I

¾ ounce lime juice

½ ounce simple syrup

1 ounce vodka

3 ounces cream soda

1 ounce dark rum

1 cocktail cherry

I. In a cocktail shaker, combine lime juice, simple syrup, and vodka. Add ice and shake for 15 seconds.

2. Strain into a collins glass over your favorite ice and add cream soda.

3. Float dark rum on top (the darkest rum you can find). Garnish with cocktail cherry.

═ Floating a Liquor ═

Floating a type of alcohol on top of a drink is a fairly simple bartending technique. First, hold a bar spoon upside down over the drink, resting the tip on the inner edge of the glass. Slowly pour the liquor you wish to float over the spoon. It will slowly cascade into the glass. Remove the spoon as the glass fills.

LAST WORD

★ ★ ★

This beautiful and herbaceous cocktail stems from the Prohibition days of *1923* and would have been a suitable drink for Arthur to savor in Season 1, Episode 8 before recklessly challenging Spencer to a duel over losing his fiancée, Alex, to him. When Arthur cowardly pulls a pistol after losing the duel, Spencer throws him overboard. This classic cocktail is also known for its ability to pack a punch while keeping balance. Fortunately, it won't leave you all wet.

— Serves I —

¾ ounce lime juice
¾ ounce Luxardo
¾ ounce gin
¾ ounce Chartreuse
1 Luxardo cherry

In a cocktail shaker, add lime juice, Luxardo, gin, and Chartreuse. Add ice and shake for 20 seconds. Strain into a coupe glass and garnish with cherry.

═ Chill Your Glass ═

Before making the drink, some bartenders will chill the glass so the cocktail will remain colder longer. If a drink sits too long before reaching its intended imbiber, the drink is sometimes referred to as having "melted."

MONTANA SOUR

★ ★ ★

Out at the camp in *Yellowstone*, the Duttons enjoy the raw scenic beauty of Montana by day, fun in the walls of their tents by night. For example, when Lynelle comes to camp to talk business with Kayce about being livestock commissioner, she ends up spending the night in John's tent. The only thing that might perfectly match such a business and pleasure day would be this beautiful sour.

───────────── **Serves I** ─────────────

1 large egg white (careful not to get any yolk in the mix, as it will destroy the texture)

3/4 ounce lemon juice

1/2 ounce huckleberry syrup

1/4 ounce elderberry liqueur

2 ounces gin

2 drops each Peychaud's and Angostura bitters

I. Combine egg white, lemon juice, huckleberry syrup, elderberry liqueur, and gin in a cocktail shaker and dry shake for 20 seconds. Add ice and shake again for 15 seconds before straining into a coupe glass.

2. Garnish by adding 2 drops of each bitter on the foamy surface of the drink, and with a toothpick, create a simple design by drawing the toothpick across the bitter drops.

Huckleberry Syrup

Huckleberry syrup can be found at your local supermarket or online. It is difficult to make yourself because of the limited availability of fresh huckleberries.

⭐

═ Egg White Cocktails ═

Using egg whites in cocktails goes back to 1862. The primary reason for using egg whites is for texture, but it also helps the overall presentation by bonding the liquids and dressing the surface of the drink with egg white topper. If you were drinking cocktails in the 1970s, chances are the whiskey sours were made with store-bought sour mix that contained no egg whites. Older folks who grew up in decades prior to the seventies most likely found it strange to be served nonfrothy sours. In more recent years, a younger generation of bartenders rediscovered and brought back the original recipes for sour drinks, which include egg whites. Like the old-fashioned and Manhattan, the original whiskey sour is one of the few cocktails enjoyed by the younger and older generations alike. Here are some useful tips to keep in mind when approaching egg white cocktails:

- **Dry shaking:** *"Dry shaking" is a term used in cocktail making that refers to shaking a drink without first adding ice. For all egg white cocktails, dry shake the drink first for 20–30 seconds. You want to build a thick layer of foam.*

- **For help shaking (a tip for those who may lack Rip's upper-body punch):** *A Hawthorne strainer is the strainer that comes with a spring attached by two prongs. Removing the spring and placing it in the shaker before shaking a drink speeds up the process and means less vigor is required to obtain the desired result.*
- **Using bitters as aromatics and garnish:** *For nearly all egg white cocktails, there's an option to drop bitters on the top of the egg white canvas and then either swirl them or line them. To do this, use a skewer or tooth-pick. Gather a drop's worth of boldly colored bitters (Angostura or Peychaud's, for example) on the end of the pick and drop it onto the cocktail's egg white top. Take the other end of the skewer and distort the drop in a design of your choice.*

BLACKBERRY BRAMBLE

★ ★ ★

In Episode 2 of *1883*, while picking blackberries, Elsa comes across a German woman who has become sick from the river water. In this case, a strong bramble with fresh berries would have been a better option to drink.

Serves I

6 blackberries, divided

¾ ounce lemon juice

¾ ounce cayenne honey syrup (see Cowboy Julep in this chapter)

2 ounces gin

I. Muddle 4 blackberries in the bottom of a cocktail shaker. Add lemon juice, cayenne honey syrup, and gin. Add half the amount of ice that would otherwise be poured into a rocks glass, shake for 15 seconds, and then pour the drink into the rocks glass.

2. Top the glass with ice, and then pour or "roll" the drink back into the shaker, then again back into the glass. Garnish with remaining 2 blackberries.

The Peasant's Pour

The "peasant's pour" is one of many names referring to a cocktailing technique that involves pouring the shaken ice and its contents directly into the serving glass, as opposed to straining the cocktail over fresh ice. In more modest bars, it saves ice and the legs of your barback, but the technique is also used for select cocktail combinations in serious bar programs.

★

≡ Death upon the Trail ≡

Though many immigrants heading west on the pioneer trails feared the Native Americans, the biggest dangers were actually disease and accidents. Due to the abysmal hygienic conditions, rampant disease killed about one in ten travelers. The most fatal was cholera, caused by consuming stagnant or unboiled water. This is why in 1883, Episode 3, Shea and Thomas made such a point about boiling the water before drinking it. Other common dangers included falling off wagons, getting crushed under the wheels, and accidental shootings. Wagon trains were armed to the teeth for fear of attack by Native Americans, but accidental discharges killed and maimed far more travelers.

LOG AND SOD

★ ★ ★

When giving Banner a house in the city in Season 1, Episode 5 of *1923*,
Donald Whitfield explains, "Cities are the mastery of one's surroundings,
and precious resources become an afterthought. No more log and sod for you."
This elevated drink would be right at home in the fanciest city house.

Serves 1

4 slices strawberry, divided

4 fresh basil leaves, divided

¾ ounce Demerara syrup

¾ ounce lemon juice

2 ounces rum

1. In a cocktail shaker, muddle 3 strawberry slices and 3 basil leaves. Add Demerara syrup, lemon juice, and rum. Add ice and shake for 15 seconds.

2. Double strain over a large ice cube in a rocks glass. Garnish with remaining strawberry slice and basil leaf.

CHAPTER 3

BEER & WINE COCKTAILS

Beer and wine have fueled the American story. Throughout this country's history, immigrants have brought their deeply rooted traditions from home, and that includes good beer and wine.

The history of these drinks also reflects our communal past. In a time when water was dangerous to drink, and cholera killed early settlers by the thousands, even children were given alcohol at an early age for hydration, nourishment, and medicine.

We now live in an exciting time for beer and wine cocktails. There have never been so many interesting beers and wines available. The world of beers alone has gone through so much transformation with craft and independent breweries popping up all over the country, each one creating their own takes on this classic beverage.

Wines also offer an immense range of possibilities—from dark, sweet ports to bubbly moscatos and dry chardonnays. Each offers unique qualities, and they lend themselves to simple, authentic drinks that calm the nerves and smooth the ride ahead.

RATTLESNAKE BITE

★ ★ ★

Episode 9 of *1883* starts off with an ominous tone as a large rattlesnake bites Risa's horse. It bucks her off it and throws her onto her back. Making matters even worse, Josef is bitten in the leg as well when he rushes to her side. This take on the snakebite cocktail adds a little tequila venom for a good sting. Maybe not enough to take down a horse, but enough to leave you smiling.

Serves 1

1 ounce lemon juice

1 ounce cinnamon honey syrup

1 ounce tequila

6 ounces hard apple cider

6 ounces Guinness

1 apple slice

1. In a pint glass, add lemon juice, cinnamon honey syrup, tequila, and hard apple cider.

2. Layer the Guinness on top of the drink by slowly pouring it over an inverted bar spoon. Garnish with apple slice.

Cinnamon Honey Syrup

To make the cinnamon honey syrup: In a small saucepan over medium heat, add equal parts honey and water. Add ground cinnamon to taste (roughly ¼ teaspoon per half cup liquid). Simmer for 2 minutes and then allow to cool.

WED AT SEA

★ ★ ★

In Season 1, Episode 6 of *1923*, Alex and Spencer are rescued after their tugboat collides with a ship and capsizes. Captain Shipley marries them, giving Alex his wife's ring and Spencer one that belonged to a dead sailor. Afterward, Alex and Spencer are offered whiskey and champagne in their quarters. This drink marries the whiskey and champagne for an effervescent celebratory drink.

— Serves I —

2 dashes orange bitters

½ ounce oloroso sherry

1 ounce bourbon

5 ounces sparkling wine

1 orange and cherry flag (see sidebar)

In a coupe glass, add bitters, sherry, and bourbon. Top with sparkling wine. Garnish with orange and cherry flag.

≡ Making a Flag ≡

A "flag" garnish is one where a citrus peel and cocktail cherry are skewered together, with the peel overlapping the cherry.

BETH'S BOILERMAKER

★ ★ ★

In *Yellowstone*, Season 1, Episode 3, Dan Jenkins spots Beth at a bar and asks Alan who she is. Alan says, "Don't even think about it, Dan. She's an assassin." Dan would have been smart to take the advice, but he instead learns the hard way. The combination of a peated Scotch and a high-ABV IPA gives this killer drink just as bold a demeanor, whether your peated Scotch is Laphroaig, Ardbeg, Oban, or otherwise.

Serves I

½ ounce rosemary syrup
¾ ounce lemon juice
1½ ounces peated Scotch
2–3 ounces IPA beer, to fill
1 rosemary sprig
1 lemon wheel

I. Chill a collins glass with ice.

2. Pour rosemary syrup, lemon juice, and Scotch into a cocktail shaker and cover with ice. Shake for 15–20 seconds, then strain into the glass over fresh ice of your preferred type.

3. Top with your favorite IPA beer. Garnish with rosemary sprig and lemon wheel.

Make Your Own Rosemary Syrup

To make rosemary syrup, combine 1 cup white sugar and 1 cup water in a small saucepan over medium heat. Add a rosemary sprig into the mix. Simmer 2–3 minutes until sugar has completely dissolved. Let cool before using and leave the sprig in while cooling.

★ A Word on Boilermakers ★

There are many origin stories around the beer and shot combo referred to as a "boilermaker." A cultural comradery surrounds the ceremonial pairing of a shot and a beer, as common today as it was throughout the early American West. Many traditions and occasions might call for a boilermaker. It's simple, it's edgy, and it's not for the faint of heart. Boilermakers have the fabric and grit of nostalgia and a cautionary tale all in one. They're usually consumed one of three ways:

1. *Shoot the whiskey, chug the beer.*

2. *Drop the whiskey-filled shot glass into the beer and then down the whole drink in one go.*

3. *Shoot the whiskey, sip the beer.*

COWBOY HAT

★ ★ ★

In Season 1, Episode 8 of *Yellowstone*, the Bunkhouse boys are drinking
beer and playing poker when Jimmy confronts them about his missing hat.
He's pleasantly surprised when they give him a brand-new one, but when
he puts it on his bed, he's quickly told never to do so, as it's bad luck.
When Jimmy asks how to undo the bad luck, Walker says, "If you cowboy
into this outfit, you're already cursed." Maybe so, but it's nothing
this cocktail can't fix. Or come close to fixing.

──────────────── Serves I ────────────────

2 thinly sliced lime wheels

½ ounce lime juice

½ ounce agave

2 dashes Peychaud's bitters

1 ounce tequila

4 ounces prosecco

I. Fill a collins glass with your preferred ice and slide
the lime wheels inside the glass so they're offset and
stacked.

2. Add lime juice, agave, bitters, and tequila and stir.
Top with prosecco.

★

═ Use Caution ═

*Be careful when adding the sparkling wine to this drink,
due to its volatile nature when added to fresh lime juice.
Slow and steady pouring is the key to keeping this drink
from overflowing.*

★ The Ranch

The Dutton Ranch barn on Yellowstone *is in fact a 6,000-square-foot log cabin located in Darby, Montana. When not home to the Duttons and all their drama, the Chief Joseph Ranch is a working ranch that includes several other cabins, including the one John gifts to Rip. Though the main lodge is a private residence, the other cabins are available to rent starting at $1,400 per night. Previously known as the Ford-Hollister Ranch, it was built over three years starting in 1914 with the intention of being one of the great log cabins in the American West. Purchased by the glass tycoon William S. Ford, the ranch was originally an apple orchard, but the trees were replaced with a massive herd of Holstein dairy cattle. Fittingly, the ranch also sits along the Lewis and Clark Trail and was first settled in 1880—not far off from when James and Margaret Dutton settled the land in the series* 1883.

CHAMPAGNE COCKTAIL

★ ★ ★

In Season 1, Episode 3 of *Yellowstone*, Beth marks the anniversary of her mom's death by drinking champagne while naked in a horse trough. Needless to say, her actions make everyone on the ranch a little uncomfortable, especially Lynelle, who spent the night with John. This cocktail can be enjoyed nude in a trough, sure, but it's even better as a celebratory drink shared with friends.

─── **Serves I** ───

2 dashes Angostura bitters

1 ounce cognac or Armagnac

1/4 ounce Demerara syrup

1 lemon peel

4–5 ounces champagne (or sparkling wine), to fill

1. In a flute glass, combine bitters, cognac or Armagnac, and Demerara syrup.

2. Twist lemon peel into the glass. *Carefully* top with champagne.

★

═ Drink Notes ═

The combination of bitters and the oil from the twist can cause the sparkling wine to quickly bubble up. The trick to finishing this drink with the sparkling wine is a slow, steady pour. A more classic take uses a sugar cube instead of a syrup. Today, an establishment will usually opt for one or the other.

NOEMI'S SANGRIA

★ ★ ★

In *1883*, Noemi, a Romani immigrant who lost her husband early
into the trek out West, falls in love with Thomas. She is always keen
on serving him food. She would do well to serve him up
a fruit-forward sangria like this one.

Serves I

½ ounce pomegranate juice
½ ounce Demerara syrup
1½ ounces dark rum
5 ounces sparkling red wine
1 cocktail cherry
1 orange slice

I. Chill a rocks glass with ice and set it aside.

2. In a cocktail shaker add pomegranate juice, Demerara syrup, and rum. Add ice and shake for 15 seconds.

3. Double strain into the rocks glass over ice and top with sparkling red wine. Garnish with cherry and orange slice.

RANCH HAND SHANDY

★ ★ ★

At the governor's party at the Dutton Ranch in Season 5, Episode 1 of *Yellowstone*, Beth asks Abby why she doesn't date cowboys. Abby replies, "'Cause they'll always love the life more. And the horse more. And the job more. The rodeo more. I wanna be first." Serving this twist on the popular ranch hand cocktail to a date will surely put you first!

◆————————— **Serves 1** —————————◆

3/4 ounce American whiskey

3/4 ounce sweet vermouth

3 ounces lemonade

2 dashes aromatic bitters

8–10 ounces Coors Banquet lager, to fill

1 lemon wheel

1. In a pint glass with your preferred type of ice, add whiskey, vermouth, lemonade, and bitters. Stir for 15 seconds.

2. Top off carefully with Coors Banquet. Garnish with lemon wheel.

≡ Shandies ≡

Often, folks will drink shandies on hot summer days in the afternoon. It's also common practice to mix a shandy with cider for a different flavor profile.

WOUNDED HUNTER

★ ★ ★

In Season 1, Episode 2 of *1923*, Spencer fights and kills a leopard.
As the doctor cleans his wounds, he says, "I wish I had something for the
pain." True to form, Spencer states, "That's what the whiskey is for."
This whiskey drink will ease the pain from any big fight, or it will
simply soothe with its complex yet balanced flavor.

Serves I

1½ ounces bourbon

¾ ounce lemon juice

¾ ounce prickly pear syrup

4 ounces champagne (or sparkling wine)

1 lemon twist

I. In a cocktail shaker, add bourbon, lemon juice, and prickly pear syrup. Add ice and shake for 15 seconds.

2. Strain into a rocks glass and top with champagne. Garnish with lemon twist.

≡ Drink Tips ≡

*To make prickly pear syrup, wash 8 prickly pears and
freeze them for 48 hours. (Be careful handling prickly pears
because their tiny spines can prick you.) Set a colander
over a container where the juice can collect, then cover the
colander with cheesecloth and place the frozen pears on
the cheesecloth, letting them sit at room temperature until
the fruit expels the juice. Allow 3–6 hours for this process.
In a saucepan over medium heat, combine equal parts juice
with sugar and heat until sugar is dissolved.*

YELLOWSTONE MICHELADA

★ ★ ★

The michelada is a classic Mexican beer-based cocktail. Combining beer with tomato juice and spices, this drink is easy to love and easy to drink. Use *The Official Yellowstone Bar Book* Bloody Mary Mix (see recipe in Chapter 5 with the Yellowstone Bloody Mary) for a complex and craveable michelada.

―――――◆――――― **Serves I** ―――――◆―――――

1 teaspoon sea salt for glass rim

1 teaspoon MSG for glass rim

2 lime wedges, divided

4 ounces *The Official Yellowstone Bar Book* Bloody Mary Mix (see Chapter 5)

4 ounces pilsner

1 ounce bourbon

I. Place salt and MSG on a small, shallow plate.

2. Wet the rim of a collins glass using 1 lime wedge. Dip the wet rim into the salt and MSG mixture to coat.

3. Fill the glass with your preferred ice and add Bloody Mary Mix and pilsner. No need to stir. Garnish with remaining lime wedge. Serve bourbon on the side. You can sip, shoot, or season the drink with the bourbon as you go.

NO-FUSS NEGRONI

★ ★ ★

In the spirit of simple drinks that are both fun and cheap together, the No-Fuss Negroni is reminiscent of the Bunkhouse, where ranch hands can unwind and throw back a couple of drinks. This cocktail pays homage to the guitar-playing cowboy Walker, a complex man who's not above simple pleasures. Here's a drink that is simple to make but deceptively complex in character.

Serves I

1 (12-ounce) bottle Miller High Life

1 ounce Campari

1 orange wedge

I. Sip or pour out 1 ounce of beer from the bottle.

2. Pour Campari into the bottle.

3. Stuff orange wedge through the neck of the bottle. Place a thumb over the bottle opening and flip the bottle upside down to float wedge to the bottom of the bottle, then return the bottle to normal.

WALKERS AND WANDERERS

★ ★ ★

After Kayce supposedly drops off Walker at the train station in Season 3, Episode 8 of *Yellowstone*, Lloyd and Rip are surprised to find him singing at the bar where they're celebrating Rip's engagement with a couple of Coors Yellow Jackets. Celebrate Walker's miraculous return to life with this smooth drink.

Serves 1

½ ounce lemon juice

½ ounce agave

1 ounce Campari

1 ounce sweet vermouth

1 (12-ounce) can Coors Yellow Jacket (Coors Banquet) lager

In a pint glass, combine lemon juice, agave, Campari, and sweet vermouth. Top with Coors.

The Coors Yellow Jacket

The "Yellow Jacket" or "Yellow Belly" is the nickname for the Coors Banquet beer, popular among Rip Wheeler and his ranch hands on Yellowstone. Coors was first created by Adolph Coors in 1873 and is made with water from the Rocky Mountains. The Yellow Jacket beer is 5% ABV (alcohol by volume), unique in that it has not been pasteurized and does not contain any preservatives. For this reason, the beer must be refrigerated, or else it will spoil. This made distribution difficult in the early days and kept the beer's availability limited to a handful of Western states until the advent of refrigerated trucks in the 1950s. The beer still had not reached every state until the early 1990s. Yellow Jackets are smooth, easy drinkers and work well in boiler-makers, as they don't have a heavy or distracting flavor.

NO SUCH THING AS FAIR

★ ★ ★

In *Yellowstone*, Season 4, Episode 9, John speaks to Carter about the buffalo, and how the army wanted them gone because they wanted the Native Americans gone. That led to the buffalo on preserves and the Native Americans on reservations, which Carter says is not fair. John sagely replies, "There's no such thing as fair." This drink pairs lavender and mint and is as fair as you're going to get. Using the soda first in this recipe "charges" the drink at the bottom of the glass. As the other ingredients are added, the bubbles carbonate and "spritz" the drink from the bottom up.

Serves I

3 ounces soda water
¼ ounce lavender syrup
¼ ounce mint syrup
½ ounce lemon juice
4 ounces white wine
1 dried lavender sprig

Fill a rocks glass with ice and add soda water first, followed by lavender and mint syrups, lemon juice, and white wine. Garnish with dried lavender sprig.

★

≡ **Making Your Own Syrups** ≡

To make lavender syrup, steep 1 cup lavender tea for 10 minutes and then remove the tea bag. Combine the tea with $\frac{1}{2}$ cup honey in a small saucepan over medium heat and simmer until honey is dissolved.

To make mint syrup, combine equal parts sugar and water plus 1 cup fresh mint in a small saucepan over medium heat. Simmer 2–3 minutes until sugar has completely dissolved. Strain the contents of the pan through a strainer into a container with an additional 1 cup fresh mint in it. Let cool for 10 minutes, then strain contents through the same strainer as before. Let cool before using.

MONTH OF SUNDAYS

★ ★ ★

Beth is overly protective of her father, so in Season 4, Episode 6 of *Yellowstone*, when she finds Summer half naked in the family kitchen one morning, she stays true to character and pulls a kitchen knife on her. As Summer fends off Beth with a milk carton, John comes in and proclaims, "Well, this is a situation I couldn't have dreamed up in a month of Sundays." This floral and delicate prosecco drink would be perfect at Sunday brunch and could help smooth things over between Beth and Summer. Might take a month of Sundays, though.

Serves 1

¼ teaspoon rose water

1 ounce Byrrh Grand Quinquina

1 ounce London dry gin

3 ounces prosecco

3 ounces tonic water

1 lime wheel

1. Fill a collins glass with your preferred type of ice, then add rose water, Byrrh Grand Quinquina, and gin and gently stir for 5 seconds.

2. Top with prosecco and tonic and garnish with lime wheel.

YOU AIN'T NO COWBOY

★ ★ ★

After Jimmy falls off his horse and gets dragged by a steer in Season 1, Episode 8 of *Yellowstone*, he blames himself for ending up cursed after putting his hat on his bunk. Rip tells him, "There ain't no such thing as luck, but I sure believe in stupid because you prove it every f*ckin' day." But it's smart to try your luck with this tasty short beer.

Serves 1

---

1 egg white

1 ounce heavy cream, whipped (see sidebar)

2 ounces Licor 43

3 ounces hazy IPA

2 ounces ginger beer

1 cocktail cherry

1. Prepare the egg white and heavy cream by combining them in a cocktail shaker and dry shaking for 20 seconds.

2. In a rocks glass, combine Licor 43, IPA, and ginger beer. Layer egg white and cream on top. Garnish with cocktail cherry.

≡ Whipping the Cream ≡

It's difficult to whip a single ounce of cream so plan on whipping about three ounces and using just one ounce for this drink.

CHAPTER 4

SHOTS

The wranglers on the Dutton Ranch work hard and play hard. And after work, the playing begins, especially in the Bunkhouse—filled with card playing, hard drinking, and sh*t talking! In Season 2, Episode 1 of *Yellowstone*, Avery claims that only the women in the Bunkhouse have any balls and challenges all to a round of "cowboy poker," a game to see who can stay seated the longest as a bull charges the table. It's a game best played after a couple of shooters.

Like cowboying, shooters are all about the basics with an emphasis on strength, smoothness, and character. Combining different spirits into shooters is a great way to mesh a rowdy bunch of flavors for a fun and lively crew.

Historically, medicines were ingested in the form of small shots. Since whiskey was considered medicine, downing an ounce or two in a small glass would have allowed for quicker ingestion and pain relief. A shooter, on the other hand, is usually a more complex drink or mini cocktail intended to be taken in a single gulp. Though the words "shots" and "shooters" are often used interchangeably, this chapter is made up entirely of shooters.

BUCKLE BUNNY

★ ★ ★

In *Yellowstone*, Season 2, Episode 6, once it's clear that Jimmy is not totally useless and can rodeo, Lloyd tells him, "You'll be up to your neck in Buckle Bunnies in no time." At first Jimmy doesn't know what this means, but it becomes clear after meeting the barrel racer Mia at the rodeo in Season 3. These sweet and tangy shooters may buck like a bronco, but they taste as sweet as pound cake and sparkle like a Buckle Bunny.

Serves 6 (I-ounce shots)

2 ounces pineapple juice

2 ounces vanilla vodka

½ ounce lemon juice

½ ounce simple syrup

¼ ounce cherry juice from cocktail cherries

I. In a cocktail shaker, combine pineapple juice, vodka, lemon juice, and simple syrup. Add ice and shake for 20 seconds, then strain into six shot glasses.

2. Carefully pour cherry juice down one side of each shot glass so it layers the bottom of each glass.

ROPE WITH MAMA

★ ★ ★

When Teeter joins the boys of the Bunkhouse, all of them may have met their match, especially Colby. In Season 4, Episode 10 of *Yellowstone*, she challenges them by saying, "You gotta come up here an' rope with Mama." She's inviting and warm, but with a bit of bite— a straight shooter just like this one.

Serves 4 (1-ounce shots)

1–2 tablespoons Tajin, for glass rims

1 lime wedge

1½ ounces tequila

¾ ounce lime juice

¾ ounce agave

1. Place Tajin on a small, shallow plate.

2. Wet the rims of four shot glasses using lime wedge. Dip the wet rims into Tajin to coat.

3. In a cocktail shaker, combine tequila, lime juice, and agave. Add ice and shake for 15 seconds.

4. Strain into prepared shot glasses.

QUITE THE PICKLE

★ ★ ★

At the end of Season 4 of *Yellowstone*, Jamie finds himself in quite the pickle. As it turns out, his birth father Garrett Randall was behind the assassination attempt on John, Kayce, and Beth. And when Beth finds out, she can only assume Jamie was behind it too. She gives him three options, none of them good. This pickleback shooter comes in three parts: salty, strong, and sour. All of them good.

──────────────── **Serves 3** ────────────────

1 tablespoon smoked sea salt

1 lime wedge

3 ounces Buffalo Trace bourbon

2 1/4 ounces spicy pickle brine

1. Place salt on a small, shallow plate.

2. Wet the rims of three shot glasses with lime wedge. Dip the wet rims into salt to coat.

3. Fill the prepared shot glasses with 1 ounce bourbon each. Then fill three separate shot glasses with 3/4 ounces brine each.

4. Lick the salt, shoot the whiskey, and then shoot the brine.

═══ **Smoked Sea Salt** ═══

Use a cocktail smoker to smoke sea salt. Measure 1/4 cup fine sea salt and pour it into a Mason jar. Smoke the jar with hardwood chips of your choice, then quickly trap the smoke under the tightened lid. The longer it sits, the more smoky the salt. For the best result, expose as much of the salt's surface area as possible by laying the jar on its side.

WHITE ELEPHANT

★ ★ ★

In Episode 1 of *1883*, after arriving in Fort Worth, Texas, the Duttons find themselves in a rowdy strip of smoky saloons known as "Hell's Half Acre." It's filled with thieves, prostitutes, and threats. This simple white and smoky shot would be right at home in such a hell, but luckily, you can make it anywhere.

Serves 4 (1-ounce shots)

2 ounces mezcal

1 ounce condensed milk dilution

1 ounce maple simple syrup

Pinch fresh ground nutmeg

Combine mezcal, condensed milk dilution, and syrup in a cocktail shaker. Add ice to cover and swirl for 10 seconds. Strain into four shot glasses. Garnish with nutmeg.

★

Making Your Ingredients

To make condensed milk dilution, add 1 part condensed milk and 1 part water into a small saucepan. Place over low heat and mix until fully combined, about 1 minute. Allow to cool before using.

To make maple simple syrup, add 1 part pure maple syrup and 1 part water into a small saucepan. Place over low heat and mix until fully combined, about 1 minute. Allow to cool before using.

America's Love-Hate Relationship with Booze

Because the Founding Fathers did not include mention of alcohol in the US Constitution, individual states had to write their own laws. So how do fifty states each tackle this issue? Randomly, and with little rational thought. Unlike countries like France or Germany, where moderate drinking has always been interwoven with national identity, Americans have historically been heavy drinkers. This heavy imbibing eventually led to the temperance movement, a campaign rooted in a puritanical outlook that sought to limit alcohol consumption through "blue laws" and eventually resulted in Prohibition in the United States. Prohibition lasted for thirteen years from 1920–1933 and was by all measures a total disaster. Since then, every state has navigated its own laws. For example, in Massachusetts, establishments are prohibited from offering happy hour; in Utah, patrons are not allowed to order doubles; in North Carolina, alcohol is prohibited anytime the game of bingo is being played. In your home, the rules are yours to write.

BUFFALO RIDER

★ ★ ★

In Season 3, Episode 6 of *Yellowstone*, everyone in the Bunkhouse decides to ride Wade's buffalo. Lloyd explains that they need to rope the buffalo around the horns and then jump on. Colby takes a swig from his flask and says, "Can't be sober for this." Make these shots for your crew next time you plan something crazy.

Serves 4 (1-ounce shots)

1½ ounces vanilla bean vodka

¾ ounce lemon juice

½ ounce simple syrup

½ ounce cherry juice from cocktail cherries

1. In a cocktail shaker, combine vodka, lemon juice, and simple syrup. Add ice and shake for 15 seconds. Strain into four shot glasses.

2. Pour cherry juice down one edge of each shot glass so that it separates from the top and collects on the bottom of each now-layered glass.

MEAN MULE

★ ★ ★

Despite Kayce's spiritual relationship with the wolf, wolves present a problem for the ranchers on *Yellowstone*. In Season 2, Episode 4, when a farmer claims one of his cows is killed by a wolf, Kayce tells him to find a mean mule to put out to pasture to protect the herd.

Serves 4 (1-ounce shots)

3/4 ounce lime juice
1/2 ounce spicy honey syrup
3/4 ounce ginger liqueur
1 1/2 ounces bourbon
4 pieces candied ginger

I. In a cocktail shaker, combine lime juice, spicy honey syrup, ginger liqueur, and bourbon. Add ice and shake for 20 seconds.

2. Strain into four shot glasses and garnish with candied ginger.

Spicy Honey Syrup

You can choose from plenty of spicy honey syrups on the store shelves or you can make it at home with jalapeño. Slice 2 jalapeños and muddle them in a small saucepan. Add 1/2 cup water and 1/2 cup honey. Place over medium heat and let simmer for 2 minutes. Allow to cool. Strain the syrup to remove the muddled peppers.

SPLIT RIP

★ ★ ★

In Season 4, Episode 3 of *Yellowstone*, Rip has two shots waiting to pour into a rocks glass for Beth and asks her if it's a one-shot or a two-shot day. She replies with a grin, "It's a pour-the-bottle-in-a-bucket kind of day." Rip adds the second shot to her glass and squeezes in a lime. This double tequila with fresh lime is as sweet as Rip's gesture, splitting the tequila with mezcal for an elevated flavor.

──────────────── **Serves 2** ────────────────

½ ounce agave
¾ ounce lime juice
1 ounce tequila
1 ounce mezcal

In a cocktail shaker, combine agave, lime juice, tequila, and mezcal. Add ice and shake for 15 seconds, then strain into two rocks glasses.

★

Cowboy Camp

Whether learning to push cattle, drive a wagon train, or cross rivers on horseback, the cast members of 1883, 1923, *and* Yellowstone *spend weeks at cowboy camp to learn to portray life in the American West as authentically as possible. The camp focuses on doing real-life cowboy tasks as a team, creating chemistry among the actors and an authentic cowboy experience for the shows. Real-life cowboy Taylor Sheridan brings on a team of professionals to help train cast members. The idea is to make the actors as comfortable and proficient as possible so that their performances are not only believable, but authentic.*

WARM S'MORES SHOOTER

★ ★ ★

In Season 1, Episode 1 of *Yellowstone*, Beth and Rip are drinking Southern Comfort while watching wolves eat an elk. Rip says, "You might just cheat death yet." Beth chases off the wolves and then replies, "It's only the things I love that die, Rip. Never me.... Come think of it, I'm surprised you're still standing." Whether you're chasing wolves or just enjoying time around the campfire, this warm and boozy drink is calming and delicious... and you'll most likely stay standing too.

◆———————— **Serves 2** ————————◆

3 ounces Southern Comfort

2 dashes chocolate bitters

3 ounces hot chocolate

2 marshmallows

I. Fill two small glasses with hot water to warm them.

2. In a cocktail shaker, combine Southern Comfort, bitters, and hot chocolate. Shake for 10 seconds, being careful not to burn yourself.

3. Dump hot water out of glasses and strain drink evenly into glasses.

4. Light each marshmallow on fire and cook to your preference. Blow out the marshmallow, shoot the shooter, eat the marshmallow.

The Four Sixes Ranch

Purchased by a group including Taylor Sheridan in 2022 for a cool $320 million, the Four Sixes Ranch (6666) covers 266,000 acres across the Texas panhandle and is larger in area than San Antonio. As in Yellowstone, the ranch is a symbol of high-quality horses and cattle and has been since its founding in 1870 by Samuel "Burk" Burnett, who purchased the ranch's original hundred head of cattle branded with "6666." Today the ranch is known for training quarter horses as well as its beef cattle. The ranch is so big it even has its own store selling every-thing the cowboys that come through need.

HORSE THIEF

★ ★ ★

In *1883*, murderers and thieves are everywhere along the Oregon Trail. In Episode 9, Shea and Thomas's outfit of pioneers comes across a family of murdered Native Americans whose horses have been stolen. It looks bad and ends worse for the pioneers. These strong, balanced shooters will steel the spine for the fight ahead.

Serves 6 (1-ounce shots)

1½ ounces honey syrup (see Bee's Knees in Chapter 2)

1½ ounces lemon juice

1½ ounces gin

¾ ounce cherry Heering

1. In a cocktail shaker, combine honey syrup, lemon juice, and gin. Add ice and shake for 15 seconds.

2. Strain into six shot glasses, leaving about a ¼ inch of space in each glass.

3. Add cherry Heering to each shot glass by carefully pouring just over the lip of the rim. (This might be easiest to do from a vessel that has a pour spout, like many mixing glasses have on one side, or a Pyrex glass measuring cup.) The cherry Heering will settle on the bottom of the glasses and have a layering effect.

GUNMAN'S HAND

★ ★ ★

In Episode 2 of *1883*, Marshal Jim Courtright, alongside James, Shea, and Thomas, shoots up the bar, killing a handful of bandits. The marshal says, "If you wanna drink at the bar, drink at the bar. But if anybody here fancies himself a gunman, you're in the wrong town. There's only one killer in Forth Worth, and that's me." These shots are spicy and smoky and can calm a nervous hand.

Serves 4 (I-ounce shots)

1 tablespoon sea salt

1 lime wedge

3 slices jalapeño

¼ ounce agave

½ ounce lime juice

½ ounce Combier

2 ounces mezcal

4 slices pickled jalapeño

I. Place salt on a small, shallow plate.

2. Wet the rims of four shot glasses with lime wedge and then place the wet part into the salt to coat.

3. In a cocktail shaker, muddle jalapeño. Add agave, lime juice, Combier, and mezcal. Add ice and shake for 15 seconds.

4. Double strain into the prepared shot glasses. Garnish with pickled jalapeño.

Test That Jalapeño

Using jalapeño can be a little tricky. The heat from one pepper to the next can vary greatly. Oftentimes, you can guess the heat of a jalapeño from the smell after it's been muddled. After you muddle, carefully nose the shaker to judge before continuing. Adjust accordingly!

WHISKEY PB&J

★ ★ ★

Rip and Beth go together like PB&J—and neither would turn down a good plate of bacon or glass of whiskey. This fun and delicious cocktail is a tribute to the classic couple. And because it tastes just like a bacon, peanut butter, and jelly sandwich, it's as easy to love as Rip and Beth themselves.

Serves 4 (1-ounce shots)

2 ounces bacon-fat-washed whiskey (see Fat Washing sidebar in Chapter 1)

½ ounce peanut butter–infused raspberry liqueur

¾ ounce chilled pure maple syrup

I. In a cocktail shaker, combine whiskey and raspberry liqueur. Add ice and shake for 20 seconds.

2. Prepare three shot glasses with ¼ ounce chilled maple syrup in each glass.

3. Using the back of a bar spoon, layer the contents of the shaker on top of the maple syrup.

Making Peanut Butter–Infused Raspberry Liqueur

In a Mason jar, combine ½ ounce creamy peanut butter with 8 ounces raspberry liqueur and mix to combine. Let it rest for 1 hour.

★

≡ A Note on Whiskey ≡

Some folks often wonder what defines a whisk(e)y. To start, the spelling of "whiskey" in general is usually a mark of the spirit's country of origin. Irish "whiskey" is almost always spelled with an "e," while Scotch "whisky" forgoes it. American whiskey tends toward using an "e" as well, but there are some exceptions. Japan and Canada follow Scotland's lead and leave it out. Although different countries have different laws defining whisk(e)y, there are two general rules regarding what defines the spirit:

- *It is a grain-based distillate. That is to say, if you're drinking something called whiskey, it's understood that the mash bill consists of either barley, corn, wheat, or rye—or some combination of the four.*
- *Whiskey is not "whiskey" until it is aged for relative times in charred or toasted oak barrels.*

DEMON CHASER

★ ★ ★

In Season 1, Episode 4 of *1923*, Alex tells Spencer that she is a jealous lover and will not share him with his demons. To chase them away, she pours a couple of drinks and sits with him to open his unread letters from the war. She tells him, "No one said demon chasing should be done sober." Agreed.

Serves 3 (1-ounce shots)

1½ ounces whiskey
½ ounce apple cider vinegar
¼ ounce Tabasco sauce
3 lime wedges
3 cilantro sprigs

In a cocktail shaker, combine whiskey, vinegar, and Tabasco sauce. Add ice, shake for 20 seconds and strain into three shot glasses. Garnish each with lime wedge and cilantro sprig.

SAVANNA SCREAMER

★ ★ ★

In Season 1, Episode 3 of *1923*, Spencer and Alex's day takes a turn for the worse when an elephant attacks their motorcar. Stranded for the night, they find themselves up a tree fending off a pride of lions. The two share drinks from a small flask. These simple and strong shooters would be perfect for the occasion.

Serves 6 (I-ounce shots)

2 ounces blended Scotch

2 ounces mushroom tea

3 dashes black walnut bitters

½ ounce ginger syrup

½ ounce lemon juice

6 pieces candied ginger

I. In a cocktail shaker, combine Scotch, tea, bitters, ginger syrup, and lemon juice. Add ice and shake for 15 seconds.

2. Double strain over six shot glasses. Add candied ginger as a garnish on each glass.

☰ Making Ginger Syrup ☰

Making ginger syrup at home requires a juicer and sugar. Wash and peel the ginger before juicing. (Be a little careful around fresh ginger juice. It's incredibly potent, and as when you're handling hot peppers, you don't want to accidentally rub your eyes after it comes into contact with your hands.) Combine equal parts juiced ginger and sugar in a small saucepan and simmer over medium heat for 3 minutes or until sugar dissolves. Let syrup cool before using.

GET OFF MY PLAIN

★ ★ ★

In *1923*, just forty years after James Dutton settled the land in Montana, his brother Jacob, alongside his wife, Cara, runs the family ranch. With a drought forcing them to move the herd up into the mountains, the Duttons fight the bold Irish sheep herders who claim the land for their herd. This nod to the aviation cocktail from the early 1900s is just as bold, balancing taste and showmanship.

Serves 4 (1-ounce shots)

2 ounces gin

3/4 ounce lemon juice

1/2 ounce simple syrup

1 ounce crème de violette

4 maraschino cherries

1. In a cocktail shaker, combine gin, lemon juice, and simple syrup. Add ice and shake for 20 seconds. Strain contents evenly across four 1-ounce shot glasses.

2. Pour 1/4 ounce crème de violette just inside the rim of each glass. (The crème de violette settles on the bottom of each glass, effectively layering each shot.) Garnish with maraschino cherry.

CHAPTER 5

DIGESTIFS & APERITIFS

Drinking around meals can be risky business in *Yellowstone*—whether it's Colby commenting too honestly on Teeter's Sonofabitch Stew in the Bunkhouse or someone (Beth) making an unappetizing scene at the Dutton dinner table. Oftentimes, the best digestif in these instances is a strong glass of bourbon.

Digestifs and aperitifs are libations intended for after or before a meal. Aperitifs are intended to whet the appetite and prepare the stomach before enjoying a heavy meal, and digestifs are enjoyed after a feast to settle the stomach and help with digestion.

Drinking an aperitif before dinner awakens the palate. These alcoholic drinks tend to be on the dry side and are often served with canapés and finger foods. A digestif is enjoyed after a large meal and tends to be stronger than its before-meal cousin. Bitter drinks like Italian amari are commonly served, as their herbal base is considered good for digestion.

BOULEVARDIER

★ ★ ★

In *Yellowstone*, whiskey is the drink of choice. The classic Boulevardier is in the same family as the classic Negroni but uses whiskey instead of gin. This warming and boozy drink is perfect when enjoyed by a warm fire on a cold night. Try firing a citrus peel for good measure.

— Serves I —

1 ounce sweet vermouth

1 ounce Campari

1 ounce bourbon or rye whiskey

2 fresh orange peels, divided

I. Combine vermouth, Campari, and bourbon in a mixing glass. Add ice and stir for 15–20 seconds. Strain over a large cube of ice in a rocks glass.

2. Fire one orange peel over the glass with a match, discard the fired peel, then garnish with remaining orange peel.

Separate or Together

In busy bars, it's common to mix a Boulevardier directly in the serving glass. In more formal cocktail bars, mixing the spirits separately before straining the combination onto fresh ice is preferred.

★ Lost Arts of Mixology ≡

- **Firing a citrus peel** is something of a fading custom. To do this right, with a simple fruit peeler, peel off two long pieces of orange skin. Make sure to avoid the white rind underneath. Light a match and warm the outside of the peel with the match in one hand and the peel gripped gently between your first two fingers and your thumb. After 2–3 seconds of warming, hold the match just above the rim of the glass and squeeze the peel in the direction of the glass. If you get it just right, a little burst of flame will shoot into the glass. You can even see the remnants of the burst in a subtle rainbowlike slick on the surface of the cocktail. Garnish the cocktail with the second rind; there's no need to squeeze the second one. Use a match instead of a lighter because the additives from a butane lighter will throw off the flavors in the drink.

- ***Throwing a cocktail*** *is another older mixing technique that is making a bit of a comeback. It's a way to add air to a cocktail that would otherwise be stirred instead of shaken. A martini, for example, would be measured in a shaker rather than a mixing glass, and ice would be added. Then the bartender would long pour the martini from the shaker into another shaker, essentially suspending the liquid in a stream momentarily before it crashed into the bottom of the other tin. Throwing a drink instead of stirring it adds air, releases subtle notes, and gives a texture that would otherwise be absent if the drink was simply stirred. A drink that is "thrown" is generally thrown a half dozen times to release the bouquet and develop the texture of the cocktail.*

NEGRONI

★ ★ ★

Yellowstone is a blend of bold vistas, compelling characters, and captivating drama. This herbaceous cocktail is also bold and captivating with its dramatic red hue and its compelling blend of bitter and sweet. The Negroni is a classic that, much like the show, is all about a balance of character.

--- **Serves I** ---

1 ounce sweet vermouth

1 ounce Campari

1 ounce gin

1 orange twist

In a mixing glass, combine vermouth, Campari, and gin. Add ice and stir for 20 seconds. Strain over a large ice cube in a rocks glass and garnish with orange twist.

★

A Balanced Drink

The Negroni, which came after the Boulevardier, is part of a unique style of cocktail where there isn't a main boozy component in a cocktail that is essentially all booze. That is to say, there is no standout liquor; all the liquors play an equal role in the balance.

TUGBOAT

★ ★ ★

In *1923*, Season 1, Episode 5, "Ghost of Zebrina," Alex and Spencer hop aboard a dilapidated tugboat, piloted by its unwell captain, Lucca. In a warning of things to come, Alex states, "And we're off, no safety brief, no toast to the gods of the sea." But *you* can make a toast to smooth sailing with this sweet-yet-bitter drink.

Serves I

1 ounce sweet vermouth

1 ounce Campari

1 ounce cognac or Armagnac

1 orange twist

Combine vermouth, Campari, and cognac in a mixing glass. Add ice and stir for 20 seconds. Strain over a large cube of ice in a rocks glass and garnish with orange twist.

★

Brandy

Brandy is as strong as whiskey, and the proof/ABV of brandy must meet a criterion to legally be labeled as such. Unlike whiskey, the name "brandy" falls under the category of spirits that are distilled from fruit. Cognac, Armagnac, and calvados are all examples of brandy.

MAD DOG

★ ★ ★

In Season 3, Episode 4 of *Yellowstone*, when Ryan and the other wranglers inform California bikers that they are trespassing on the Dutton Ranch and need to move on, things become a tad combative, and when one of the women from their gang says Teeter is a pink-haired b*tch, well, that doesn't end well for the bikers, or their bikes. Like Teeter, this aperitif is pink, and demands your respect.

———————————— Serves I ————————————

½ ounce orgeat (almond syrup)

¾ ounce lemon juice

1 ounce apple brandy

¾ ounce Campari

2–3 ounces prosecco, to fill

In a mixing glass, combine orgeat, lemon juice, apple brandy, and Campari. Double strain into a rocks glass over your preferred ice. Top with prosecco.

COWBOY COFFEE

★ ★ ★

After a group of bikers are found trespassing on John's land in Season 3, Episode 4 of *Yellowstone*, a fight ensues. Knowing that the bikers will come back, John, Kayce, and Rip wait up all night for them. When they do come back, the bikers are ambushed and forced to dig their own graves. Stay up late for your next ambush with this hot, caffeinated drink—it's like an Irish coffee, but with bourbon.

———— Serves I ————

1 ounce Buffalo Trace bourbon cream

1 ounce heavy cream

2 ounces Buffalo Trace bourbon

8 ounces hot coffee

I. Prep a clear coffee cup or heatproof wine glass by filling it halfway with hot water to warm the vessel. (Only fill it halfway because you want the upper part of the glass to remain a bit cooler relative to the bottom of the glass to help keep the layers of the drink from mixing.)

2. Combine bourbon cream and heavy cream in a cocktail shaker and dry shake the two together for 20 seconds.

3. Empty hot water from the cocktail vessel. Add bourbon directly to the glass and top the glass with coffee to 3/4 inch below the rim.

4. Layer the drink with the whipped bourbon cream and heavy cream.

MARGARET'S ENVY

★ ★ ★

In Episode 4 of *1883*, Elsa tells her mom, Margaret, that she kissed Ennis and may love him: "I get butterflies when he looks at me. And when he doesn't." Margaret tells Elsa she's envious of her becoming a woman out on the trail. This hot drink with butterfly pea flower tea can bring a touch of love to any night out on the plains.

Serves I

½ ounce huckleberry syrup

1½ ounces bourbon

1 butterfly pea flower tea bag

4 ounces hot water

1 cinnamon stick

Dried clove for smoking

I. In a clear coffee mug, combine syrup, bourbon, and tea bag, then add hot water. Steep for 3–5 minutes and remove tea bag.

2. With a pastry torch, blacken cinnamon stick and drop it into the mug.

3. With a cocktail smoker, smoke the cocktail with dried clove and serve.

≡ A Color Show ≡

You can also serve this drink with a lemon wedge for a burst of flavor and to watch this blue drink turn to purple.

NECESSARY EVIL

★ ★ ★

John still holds on to the dream of having all his children living under the same roof. In Season 1, Episode 5 of *Yellowstone*, "Coming Home," Beth takes up residence at the Dutton Ranch. It's not exactly a peaceful fulfillment of John's wish; as he drinks with his son Jamie in the living room, they can hear her screaming in a drunken rage. Jamie, contending for more responsibility, tells his father, "I can do whatever she does." John replies, "She can be evil, and evil is what I need right now." If you need a little evil in your life, raise a glass of this drink.

Serves I

1 ounce Dolin sweet vermouth

1 ounce Campari

1 ounce Laird's applejack

1 orange twist

Combine vermouth, Campari, and applejack in a mixing glass. Add ice and stir for 15 seconds. Strain over a large ice cube in a rocks glass and garnish with orange twist.

★

Applejack

Applejack has been in America since colonial times, but William Laird is thought to have been the first to bring this spirit to market in 1698. Laird's distillery is said to be the oldest in the United States.

BIG SKY

★ ★ ★

In *1883*, Episode 8, Elsa narrates: "The plains are for the vagabonds, wanderers, and cowboys. Their home is a saddle, the sky is their roof, the ground is their bed. What they lack in material comfort is regained in the knowledge that they are always home. To them, the journey is the destination." This drink is just as poetic as anything Elsa ever said about Big Sky Country.

Serves I

1 ounce brewed and chilled butterfly pea flower tea

1 ounce Dolin blanc vermouth

1 ounce Cocchi Americano

1 ounce St. George Terroir gin

1 blood orange wheel

I. In a mixing glass, combine tea, vermouth, Cocchi Americano, and gin. Add ice and stir 20 seconds.

2. Strain into a coupe glass and garnish with blood orange wheel.

ON THE MEND

★ ★ ★

For every generation of Dutton, whether pioneer, lawman, or landowner, life comes with risk. Just about every Dutton has taken a bullet or an arrow while upholding the burden of duty. And just about every Dutton fights on until they are on the mend. This warm, healing elixir of brandy, whiskey, and ginger is a tried-and-true remedy with a sweet finish for easy consumption.

───────────────── **Serves I** ─────────────────

¾ ounce ginger syrup (see Savanna Screamer in Chapter 4)

⅛ ounce almond extract

1 ounce whiskey

1 ounce sweet vermouth

1 ounce apple brandy

2 cinnamon sticks, divided

I. Add ginger syrup, almond extract, whiskey, vermouth, and brandy to a small saucepan.

2. Add 1 cinnamon stick and simmer over low heat for 5 minutes.

3. Remove from heat and strain into a warm mug. Garnish with remaining cinnamon stick.

RAINWATER

★ ★ ★

In Season 1, Episode 4 of *1923*, after endless abuse by Sister Mary and Sister Alice at the boarding school, Teonna Rainwater wages war. She kills them both, with historic weight and poetic justice, resulting in one of the most poignant scenes of the series. Like Teonna, this aromatic drink is complex with a bitter streak.

Serves I

1 ounce Lillet blanc
1½ ounces Suze gentian liqueur
3 ounces prosecco
1 long orange twist

In a flute glass, add Lillet and Suze. Top with prosecco and garnish with orange twist.

≡ Suze ≡

Suze, a French aperitif, has been on the market since 1889. The gentian component of this liqueur has been used in traditional medicine for centuries. Having a bitter and herbal quality, the elixir is touted to be a cure-all for everything from headaches to stomach issues.

VIEUX CARRÉ

★ ★ ★

In Season 3, Episode 5 of *Yellowstone*, Beth is at the bar, characteristically drinking whiskey. As he passes, Roarke takes the opportunity to confront her about shorting his stock. "Why are you poking a grizzly?" Beth asks. "You are the trailer park. I am the tornado." It's a classic, self-knowing line. Likewise, this classic, split-based drink knows itself as a stomach-settling blend of rye and cognac.

───────────────── **Serves I** ─────────────────

1 ounce rye whiskey

1 ounce cognac

1 ounce sweet vermouth

1 teaspoon Bénédictine

2 dashes Peychaud's bitters

1 cocktail cherry

I. Add all ingredients except cherry to a mixing glass. Add ice and stir for 15–20 seconds.

2. Strain into a rocks glass over your preferred ice. Garnish with cherry.

═ A Stomach Settler ═

The Vieux Carré originated in New Orleans and is a great option for before or after dinner. This classic drink is boozy and complex and has subtle herbal notes that will prep or settle the stomach pre- or post-meal.

BROKEN ROCK FIZZ

★ ★ ★

In Season 1, Episode 2 of *Yellowstone*, Chief Rainwater tells Kayce, "There's no such thing as a good man. All men are bad. But some of us try real hard to be good." The bitterness and dryness of amaro and sherry try to take over in this aperitif, but the bright burst of citrus and bubbles in the lemon seltzer keeps things balanced and smooth.

Serves I

1 ounce fino sherry

1 ounce amaro

6 ounces lemon seltzer

1 lemon twist

1. Fill a collins glass with your preferred ice, then add fino sherry and amaro.

2. Top with lemon seltzer. Stir to combine ingredients. Garnish with lemon twist.

Setting the Stage for the Golden Age of Cocktails

The word "cocktail" with its current definition was first seen in print in 1806, and the first known collection of alcoholic beverage recipes was put together by students at Oxford in 1827. Although cocktails certainly had been around to some degree, they wouldn't become a ubiquitous part of American bar culture for several more decades. One of the factors that set the stage for the "Golden Age" was an influx of immigrants into the United States. The mass migration into the United States from central Europe was made possible due to the change from sail to steam technology. Consequently, passage was cheaper and safer, and it took much less time to cross shipping lanes throughout various transatlantic passages. European immigrants in the US brought with them a drinking culture, and at the same time, the US government decreased taxes on alcohol. The Industrial Revolution was also well underway, and as a result, basic goods had become much more affordable. The final ingredient that spurred on the cocktail boom was a bartender named Jerry Thomas, who in 1862 published the Bar-Tender's Guide. *Thomas's publication brought otherwise guarded cocktail recipes to the public light, and consequently, cocktail culture exploded.*

YELLOWSTONE BLOODY MARY

★ ★ ★

The Bloody Mary is perfect for day drinking, a popular habit among the Dutton family. It's also a great drink to embellish with your favorite ingredients and toppings. This version of the classic uses smoked sea salt and fat-washed bourbon to stand out.

Serves I

½ ounce smoked sea salt, for glass rim (see Quite the Pickle in Chapter 4)

½ ounce MSG, for glass rim

1 lime wedge

2 ounces bacon-fat-washed bourbon (see Fat Washing sidebar in Chapter 1)

8 ounces *The Official Yellowstone Bar Book* Bloody Mary Mix (see recipe that follows)

1 piece candied bacon

1 medium stalk celery

1 skewer blue cheese–stuffed olives and watermelon cubes

I. Place salt and MSG on a small, shallow plate.

2. Wet the rim of a collins glass with lime wedge. Dip the wet rim into salt and MSG to coat.

3. Fill the glass with your preferred ice. Add bourbon and Bloody Mary Mix. Stir.

4. Garnish with candied bacon, celery, and skewered olives and watermelon.

THE OFFICIAL
YELLOWSTONE BAR BOOK
BLOODY MARY MIX

★ ★ ★

Makes about 1 quart

2$\frac{1}{2}$ cups tomato juice

$\frac{1}{2}$ cup Spicy Hot V8

1$\frac{1}{2}$ ounces Worcestershire sauce

$\frac{3}{4}$ ounce lemon juice

$\frac{3}{4}$ ounce lime juice

$\frac{1}{2}$ cup Coors Yellow Jacket

$\frac{1}{2}$ teaspoon MSG

$\frac{1}{2}$ teaspoon salt

$\frac{1}{2}$ teaspoon ground black pepper

$\frac{1}{8}$ cup prepared horseradish

$\frac{1}{8}$ cup spicy pickle juice

$\frac{1}{8}$ cup olive brine

$\frac{1}{8}$ cup red wine vinegar

Mix all ingredients together in an airtight container. Store in the refrigerator up to 5 days.

OLD AND RUSTY

★ ★ ★

Ranch hands come and go on *Yellowstone*, but Rip and Lloyd are in it for life.
In Season 2, Episode 2, Rip tells Lloyd, "It's just a reminder—they might let
us stay here and get old and rusted, but we're just tools, and that's all
we'll ever be." This drink looks old and rusty but will restore
your usefulness after a heavy meal.

Serves I

⅛ ounce pure vanilla extract

½ ounce orgeat (almond syrup)

2 dashes Peychaud's bitters

1½ ounces sweet vermouth

1½ ounces gin

1 lemon twist

Combine vanilla extract, orgeat, bitters, vermouth, and gin in a mixing glass. Add ice of your choice and stir for 20 seconds. Strain into a coupe glass and garnish with lemon twist.

About the Authors

Lex and Nathan both share a profound love of the outdoors—from hunting and fishing to hiking and canoeing to survival and bushcraft. Their adventures and interests cover a lot of territory. Together, they have paired up to share their deep knowledge of spirits and drinks as well as their love of the land and the roots of America. As huge *Yellowstone* fans, they tell this story through the themes and characters they love…and love to hate.

Lex Taylor is an author, chef, outdoorsman, bushcrafter, forager, knife maker, leather smith, and adventurer. He is the winner of Esquire's *The Next Great Burger* and has been featured on Food Network shows. Lex is a barbecue pitmaster and outdoor chef and hosts wilderness dinners and cocktail pairings that celebrate nature with wild ingredients. He has published two cookbooks that look at wilderness ingredients, live-fire cooking, international flavors, and cocktails. Lex studies traditional knowledge and has adventured across the world and the Americas from the Atacama Desert in Chile to the Canadian Arctic. He has lived and hunted with the Inuit of Baffin Island and is a member of The Explorers Club. Find him on Instagram at @The.North.Feast.

Nathan Gurr is a cocktail and spirits expert, seasoned barman, woodworker, avid outdoorsman, and lifelong learner. Specializing in American whiskeys and cocktails, Nathan develops bar programs for acclaimed establishments across New York State, including extensive tenures as beverage director for both Todd English and the Zabar family, and most recently at Whiskey River in Peekskill, New York, which was awarded Best Whiskey Program in Westchester County by *Westchester Magazine* in 2024. His expertise is sought by both private and commercial clients, crafting whiskey tastings and curating private collections for both the private and commercial sectors. Nathan has been featured in *Forbes*, *Men's Health*, *GQ*, and *Time Out*, and in *UPROXX* among industry legends Jimmy and Eddie Russell for their take on the US bourbon boom.

Index

A

Absinthe
    about: Sazerac and, 60
    Knife's Tip, 49
Accessorizing cocktails, 42–43
Alcohol. *See also* Cocktails; *specific alcohols*
    America's love-hate relationship with booze and, 144
    "Golden Age" of cocktails and, 193
Amaro
    Broken Rock Fizz, 192
    Heartless Cowgirl, 54–55
Americano, in Big Sky, 184–85
Aperitifs. *See* Digestifs and aperitifs
Apple brandy
    Mad Dog, 176
    On the Mend, 187
Apple cider, hard, in Rattlesnake Bite, 102–3
Applejack, in Necessary Evil, 183
Armagnac
    about: brandy and, 175
    Cowboy Hat, 109
    Iron in the Fire, 41
    Tugboat, 175

B

Bacon, fat washing booze and, 24. *See also* Fat-washed booze

Bar spoon, 9
Bar tools, 9–11
Beer
    about: Coors "Yellow Jacket" or "Yellow Belly," 125; wine and, in drinks, 99, 101 (*See also* Wine)
    Beth's Boilermaker, 107–8
    No-Fuss Negroni, 123
    Ranch Hand Shandy, 116
    Rattlesnake Bite, 102–3
    Walkers and Wanderers, 124–25
    Yellowstone Michelada, 120–21
    You Ain't No Cowboy, 130–31
Bee's Knees, 70–71
Beet juice ice cubes, 79
Beth's Boilermaker, 107–8
Beth's Martini, 31
Big Sky, 184–85
Bitters
    about, 41
    as aromatics and garnishes, 93
    egg white cocktails and, 93
Blackberry Bramble, 94–95
Bloody Mary
    The Official Yellowstone Bar Book Bloody Mary Mix, 196
    Yellowstone Bloody Mary, 194–95
Boilermakers
    about: Coors "Yellow Jacket" or "Yellow Belly" and, 125; origins and consumption options, 108

Beth's Boilermaker, 107
Boulevardier, 168–69
Bourbon. *See also* High-rye bourbon
    about: Buffalo Trace bourbon, 83;
    fat washing, 24; Weller Special
    Reserve bourbon, 21, 83
    Boulevardier, 168–69
    Bourbon Buck, 47
    Classic Manhattan, 27
    Classic Old-Fashioned, 18–19
    Cowboy Coffee, 178–79
    Iron in the Fire, 41
    Manhattan's Black Heart, 28–29
    Margaret's Envy, 180–81
    Mean Mule, 147
    Pioneer Old-Fashioned, 22–25
    Quite the Pickle, 140–41
    Starry Night (high-rye bourbon),
    62–63
    Sting of Wisdom, 73
    Wed at Sea, 104–5
    Yellowstone Bloody Mary, 194–95
    Yellowstone Michelada, 120–21
    Yellowstone Ranch Old-Fashioned,
    21
Branding cattle, 44
Brandy, about, 175. *See also*
    Armagnac; Cognac
Broken Rock Fizz, 192
Buck, bourbon, 47
Buckle Bunny, 136–37
Buffalo Rider, 145
    Wounded Hunter, 119
Buffalo Trace bourbon, 83
Buffalo Trace White Dog, in Heartless
    Cowgirl, 54–55
Building cocktails, 42–43
Buster Welch, 48

C

Camp, cowboy, 149
Campari
    Boulevardier, 168–69
    Necessary Evil, 183
    Negroni, 173
    No-Fuss Negroni, 123
    Tugboat, 175
    Walkers and Wanderers, 124–25
Cara's Threat, 74–75
Carolyn's Whiskey Punch, 56–57
Cattle, branding, 44
Cayenne Honey Syrup, 82
Champagne. *See* Wine
Charcoal, activated, 28
Chartreuse, in Last Word, 88–89
Chief Joseph Ranch, 111
Chilling glasses, 88
Chocolate, in Warm S'mores Shooter,
    150–51
Cinnamon Honey Syrup, 102
Citrus peel, firing, 170
Classic Bee's Knees, 71
Classic Manhattan, 27
Classic Modern Daiquiri, 76–77
Classic Old-Fashioned, 18–19
Cocktails. *See also* Beer; Digestifs and
    aperitifs; Shaken cocktails; Shots;
    Stirred cocktails; Wine; *specific
    alcohol main ingredients*; *specific
    cocktail names*
    about: this book and, 7
    bar tools for making, 9–11
    bitters and, 41
    building, dressing, and
        accessorizing, 42–43
    chilling glasses, 88

egg whites in, 92–93 (*See also* Egg white cocktails)
flag garnishes, 104
floating a liquor, 87
glasses for, 11–13
"Golden Age" of, 193
Jerry Thomas and, 193
lost arts of mixology, 170–71
origins of, 193
"peasant's pour," 94
"Prohibition Cocktails," 71
rolling, 52
smoking, 10, 43
throwing (technique), 171
Yellowstone, spin-off series *1883*, *1923* and, 17
Coffee, cowboy, 178–79
Cognac
    about: brandy and, 175
    Cowboy Hat, 109
    Tugboat, 175
    Vieux Carré, 190–91
Collins glasses, 11
Condensed milk dilution, 143
Coupe glasses, 11
Cowboy camp, 149
Cowboy Coffee, 178–79
Cowboy Hat, 109
Cowboy Julep, 82–83
Cowboys and Dreamers, 68
Cream, whipping, 130

D

Daiquiri, Classic Modern, 76–77
Death upon the trail, 96
Demon Chaser, 159

Digestifs and aperitifs, 164–97
    about: a balanced drink, 173; definitions and purposes of, 167
    Big Sky, 184–85
    Boulevardier, 168–69
    Broken Rock Fizz, 192
    Cowboy Coffee, 178–79
    Mad Dog, 176
    Margaret's Envy, 180–81
    Necessary Evil, 183
    Negroni, 173
    The Official Yellowstone Bar Book Bloody Mary Mix, 196
    Old and Rusty, 197
    On the Mend, 187
    Rainwater, 188
    Tugboat, 175
    Vieux Carré, 190–91
    Yellowstone Bloody Mary, 194–95
Double rocks glasses, 12
Dressing cocktails, 42–43
Dutton Ranch, buildings and history, 111

E

Egg white cocktails
    about, 92–93; bitters as aromatics and garnishes, 93; history of, 92; shaking and dry shaking, 93
    Montana Sour, 90–93
    You Ain't No Cowboy, 130–31

F

Fat-washed booze
    about: fat washing, 24
    Pioneer Old-Fashioned, 22–23
    Whiskey PB&J, 157

Yellowstone Bloody Mary, 194–95
Firing a citrus peel, 170
Flag garnish, making, 104
Floating a liquor, 87
Flute glasses, 12
Ford-Hollister Ranch, 111
Four Sixes Ranch, 152

G

Get Off My Plain, 163
Gin
    about: Gin Rickey and Bee's Knees
      as "Prohibition Cocktails," 71
    Bee's Knees, 70–71
    Big Sky, 184–85
    Blackberry Bramble, 94–95
    Cowboys and Dreamers, 68
    Get Off My Plain, 163
    Gin Rickey, 38–39
    Horse Thief, 153
    Last Word, 88–89
    Liquid Courage (gin and tonic),
      80–81
    Modern Martini, 33
    Montana Sour, 90–93
    Month of Sundays, 129
    Negroni, 173
    Old and Rusty, 197
Ginger Syrup, 160
Glasses
    chilling, 88
    types of, 11–13
"Golden Age" of cocktails, 193
Guinness syrup
    about: making, 28
    Long Black Train, 50–51
    Manhattan's Black Heart, 28–29
Gunman's Hand, 154–55

H

Hard apple cider, in Rattlesnake Bite,
  102–3
Heartless Cowgirl, 54–55
High Plains Sazerac, 59–61
Honey
    Cayenne Honey Syrup, 82
    Cinnamon Honey Syrup, 102
    Honey Syrup, 70
    Spicy Honey Syrup, 73, 147
Horse Thief, 153
Huckleberry Syrup, 90

I

Ice
    beet juice cubes, 79
    cube size advantage, 23
    molds for, 11
    "peasant's pour" and, 94
    stirred cocktails and, 17
    water and, 17
Iron in the Fire, 41

J

Jalapeño, testing heat, 154
Jigger, 9
Julep, Cowboy, 82–83

K

Knife's Tip, 49

L

Last Word, 88–89
Lavender Syrup, 128
Legality of alcohol, America and, 144
Lillet blanc, in Rainwater, 188

Liquid Courage (gin and tonic), 80–81
Log and Sod, 97
Long Black Train, 50–51

M

Manhattan
    about: on the rocks, 27
    Classic Manhattan, 27
    Manhattan's Black Heart, 28–29
Maple Simple Syrup, 143
Margaret's Envy, 180–81
Marshmallow, in Warm S'mores
  Shooter, 150–51
Marshmallow Syrup, 62
Martini glasses, 12
Martinis
    about: evolution and presentation,
      34; lingo definitions, 34–35
    Modern Martini, 33
    Phantom Pain (Beth's Martini), 31
Mean Mule, 147
Metal shakers, 9
Mezcal
    Gunman's Hand, 154–55
    Rip Roy, 44
    Split Rip, 149
    White Elephant, 143
Michelada, Yellowstone, 120–21
Mint Julep. *See* Cowboy Julep
Mint Syrup, 128
Mixing glass, 9
Mixology, lost arts of, 170–71
Modern Martini, 33
Molds, ice, 11
Montana Sour, 90–93
Month of Sundays, 129

Moonshine, in Heartless Cowgirl,
  54–55
Mugs, 12

N

Necessary Evil, 183
Negroni, 173
    No-Fuss Negroni, 123
Noemi's Sangria, 115
No-Fuss Negroni, 123
No Such Thing as Fair, 126–28

O

Old and Rusty, 197
Old-fashioned
    about: fat washing booze and, 22,
      24; large ice cubes for, 23;
      varying the drink, 18
    Classic Old-Fashioned, 18–19
    Yellowstone Ranch Old-Fashioned,
      21
Olive oil, quality of, 68
On the Mend, 187

P

Pastry torch, 10
PB&J, Whiskey, 157
Peanut Butter–Infused Raspberry
  Liqueur, 157
"Peasant's pour," 94
Phantom Pain (Beth's Martini), 31
Pickleback shooter, 140–41
Pint glasses, 12
Pioneer Old-Fashioned, 22–25
Prickly Pear Syrup, 119
Prize Fighter, 79

Prohibition, historical perspective, 144
"Prohibition Cocktails," 71
Prosecco. *See* Wine
Punch, Carolyn's Whiskey Punch, 56–57

Q

Quite the Pickle, 140–41

R

Ranches
    Dutton Ranch, buildings and history, 111
    Four Sixes Ranch, 152
Ranch Hand Shandy, 116
Ranch Water, 36–37
Raspberry liqueur, peanut butter–infused, 157
Rattlesnake Bite, 102–3
Rip Roy (take on classic Rob Roy), 44
Rocks glasses, 13
Rolling a cocktail, 52
Root beer, drugstore, 52–53
Rope with Mama, 138–39
Rosemary Syrup, 107
Rum
    Classic Modern Daiquiri, 76–77
    Log and Sod, 97
    Spicy Summer, 84
Rum (dark)
    about: changing to change cocktail's flavor, 76
    Drugstore Root Beer, 52
    Noemi's Sangria, 115
    Twister, 87

Rye whiskey. *See also* High-rye bourbon
    Boulevardier, 168–69
    High Plains Sazerac, 59–61
    Long Black Train, 50–51
    Vieux Carré, 190–91

S

Salt (sea), smoking, 140
Sangria, Noemi's, 115
Sazerac
    about: history of, 60
    High Plains Sazerac, 59–61
Scotch
    Beth's Boilermaker, 107–8
    Rip Roy, 44
    Savana Screamer, 160
Shaken cocktails, 64–97
    about: shaking, 67
    Bee's Knees, 70–71
    Blackberry Bramble, 94–95
    Cara's Threat, 74–75
    Classic Modern Daiquiri, 76–77
    Cowboy Julep, 82–83
    Cowboys and Dreamers, 68
    Last Word, 88–89
    Liquid Courage, 80–81
    Log and Sod, 97
    Montana Sour, 90–93
    Prize Fighter, 79
    Spicy Summer, 84
    Sting of Wisdom, 73
    Twister, 87
Shakers, 9
Shandy, Ranch Hand, 116
Sheridan, Taylor, 49, 149, 152
Sherry, in Broken Rock Fizz, 192

Shot glass, 13
Shots, 132–63
    about: America's love-hate relation-
        ship with booze and, 144; history
        of, 135
    Buckle Bunny, 136–37
    Buffalo Rider, 145
    Demon Chaser, 159
    Get Off My Plain, 163
    Gunman's Hand, 154–55
    Horse Thief, 153
    Mean Mule, 147
    Quite the Pickle, 140–41
    Rope with Mama, 138–39
    Savana Screamer, 160
    Split Rip, 149
    Warm S'mores Shooter, 150–51
    Whiskey PB&J, 157
    White Elephant, 143
Smoked sea salt, 140
Smoked syrups, 43
Smoker (wood chip) and
    wood chips, 10
Smoking cocktails, 10, 43
S'mores shooter, warm, 150–51
Sparkling wine. See Wine
Spicy Honey Syrup, 73, 147
Spicy Summer, 84
Split Rip, 149
Spoon, bar, 9
Starry Night, 62–63
Sting of Wisdom, 73
Stirred cocktails, 14–63
    about: fat washing booze and, 24;
        water, ice and, 17
    Bourbon Buck, 47
    Carolyn's Whiskey Punch, 56–57

Classic Manhattan, 27
Classic Old-Fashioned, 18–19
Drugstore Root Beer, 52
Gin Rickey, 38–39
Heartless Cowgirl, 54–55
High Plains Sazerac, 59–61
Iron in the Fire, 41
Knife's Tip, 49
Long Black Train, 50–51
Manhattan's Black Heart, 28–29
Modern Martini, 33
Phantom Pain (Beth's Martini), 31
Pioneer Old-Fashioned, 22–25
Ranch Water, 36–37
Rip Roy (take on classic Rob Roy),
    44
Starry Night, 62–63
Yellowstone Ranch Old-Fashioned,
    21
Stomach settler, 190–91. See also
    Digestifs and aperitifs
Strainer, 10
Suze gentian liqueur, in Rainwater, 188
Syrups
    about: making your own, 128;
        smoked syrups, 43
    Cayenne Honey Syrup, 82
    Cinnamon Honey Syrup, 102
    Ginger Syrup, 160
    Honey Syrup, 70
    Huckleberry Syrup, 90
    Lavender Syrup, 128
    Maple Simple Syrup, 143
    Marshmallow Syrup, 62
    Mint Syrup, 128
    Peanut Butter–Infused Raspberry
        Liqueur, 157

Prickly Pear Syrup, 119
Rosemary Syrup, 107
Spicy Honey Syrup, 73, 147

T

Tequila
    Cowboy Hat, 109
    Ranch Water, 36–37
    Rattlesnake Bite, 102–3
    Rope with Mama, 138–39
    Split Rip, 149
Thomas, Jerry, 193
Throwing a cocktail, 171
Tonics
    about: trying new tonics, 80
    Liquid Courage (gin and tonic),
      80–81
Tools, 8–13
    bar tools, 9–11
    glasses, 11–13
Torch, pastry, 10
Trail, death upon, 96
Twister, 87

V

Vanilla bean vodka,
  in Buffalo Rider, 145
Vermouth
    Big Sky, 184–85
    Boulevardier, 168–69
    Classic Manhattan, 27
    Necessary Evil, 183
    Negroni, 173
    Old and Rusty, 197
    On the Mend, 187
    Ranch Hand Shandy, 116

Rip Roy, 44
Tugboat, 175
Vieux Carré, 190–91
Walkers and Wanderers, 124–25
Vieux Carré, 190–91
Vodka
    Buckle Bunny, 136–37
    Buffalo Rider (vanilla bean vodka),
      145
    Cara's Threat, 74–75
    Cowboys and Dreamers, 68
    Phantom Pain (Beth's Martini), 31
    Prize Fighter, 79
    Twister, 87

W

Walkers and Wanderers, 124–25
Warm S'mores Shooter, 150–51
Wed at Sea, 104–5
Welch, Buster, 48
Weller Special Reserve bourbon, 21, 83
Whipping cream, 130
Whiskey. *See also* Bourbon;
  Rye whiskey; Scotch
    about, 158; aging, 158; Buffalo
      Trace whiskey, 83; spelling
      "whiskey" or "whisky," 158
    Carolyn's Whiskey Punch, 56–57
    Demon Chaser, 159
    On the Mend, 187
    Ranch Hand Shandy, 116
    Warm S'mores Shooter, 150–51
    Whiskey PB&J, 157
White Elephant, 143
Wine
    about: beer and, in drinks, 99, 101
    (*See also* Beer)

Champagne Cocktail, 112–13
Cowboy Hat, 109
Knife's Tip, 49
Mad Dog, 176
Month of Sundays, 129
Noemi's Sangria, 115
No Such Thing as Fair, 126–28
Rainwater, 188
Wed at Sea, 104–5
Wounded Hunter, 119
Wine glasses, 13
Wood chip smoker and wood chips, 10
Wounded Hunter, 119

Y

Yellowstone Bloody Mary, 194–95
Yellowstone Michelada, 120–21
Yellowstone Ranch Old-Fashioned, 21
You Ain't No Cowboy, 130–31